Abu R

Ruqya
Islamic Exorcism

Protection and Healing

-

Jinn, Sorcery and Evil Eye

Text and Cover
Abu Rayan

www.tauhd.net

Third Edition 1445

All praise and thanks are due to Allāh. We praise and give thanks to Him. We seek His aid and ask for His forgiveness, and we seek Allāh's refuge from the evil of ourselves and from our evil actions. Whomsoever Allāh guides then none can misguide him, and whomsoever He misguides then none can guide him. I bear witness that none has the right to be worshipped except Allāh, alone, having no partner, and I bear witness that Muhammad is His slave and His Messenger.

Please take notice: *This book contains verses of the Qur'an and names of Allāh in Arabic writing, therefore please do not take it into the toilet or throw it into the garbage. If it is not needed anymore, please burn it at a clean place. Thanks!*

Limited liability: *We are not liable for any damages or injuries caused by the practice of the methods mentioned in this book!*

Index

Preface

There is hardly a better opportunity for observing the power of the Qur'an than during Ruqya. With the recitation of the Qur'an alone, devils can be expelled and even killed. What might sound like a fairytale for the average Westerner is a recognized practice in Islam.

But even many Muslims do not know how many diseases and ailments are caused by Jinn! It is generally assumed that obsession is manifested by schizophrenic conditions, as in the form of a severe mental illness. These are, however, only the extreme forms and the tip of the iceberg. In fact, most people are bothered by Jinn without noticing it. If the Jinn remain in the body for a longer period, they cause most often diseases, both physical and mental.

With such diseases Western medicine is usually hopelessly overburdened. Especially in cases of "mental diseases" Western medicine can often do nothing more than immobilize the patient with severe psycho-pharmaceuticals such as Haldol. If one gets such a treatment, one has a bad chance of ever becoming "normal" again because of the serious side effects. Even in cases of diseases such as eczema and psoriasis, western medicine is generally quite helpless because it often does not recognize the true causes. Not to mention blockades in life, which are not even recognized as a medical problem!

As obvious as the symptoms are for those who know and are able to classify them, western medicine is blind to them as they dismiss Jinn as a child tale. When we read such headlines as the following, the one who is familiar with Jinn understands the causes immediately, while western medicine is left in the dark:

Düsseldorf - Sept. 5, 2017. According to a psychiatrist, the alleged amok runner at Düsseldorf's central station was acting on the orders of inner voices. They had ordered the indiscriminate attacks on travelers to provoke his killing by the police. This was reported to him by the mentally ill man in his assessment, the expert said on Tuesday at process launch.

The man will come into a secluded psychiatry, packed with psychopharmaceuticals, and will not become "normal" ever again.

Because there are not many Muslims in the West, and unfortunately, not many of them know about Ruqya, experienced healers often live far away. At the same time, however, Muslims in the West live in a non-Islamic environment that favours devils. It is therefore not surprising that there are many people who have problems and are left alone with these problems.

This book is intended to assist in both diagnosis and treatment, as well as to explain things that are generally important, e.g. daily sunnahs for protection. Treatment methods are presented which do not require any Raqi (someone who practices Ruqya), but which everybody can practice by himself with God's permission. This book will also be a useful reference to the novice Raqi. And, of course, dealing with the subject of Ruqya has many positive aspects that should result in a better understanding and practice of Islam.

It is very important to understand that if someone has a problem with Jinn, it can not be easily solved with just a Ruqya session, as if one is going to the doctor who prescribes a few pills. When such a problem occurs, it is a call from Allāh to examine one's whole life and to restructure it in many areas, since the expelling of the Jinn with Ruqya is usually only a small part of the entire healing process. The patient must find out the true causes that have led to the problem and change his life in order that he is protected in the future and the Jinn will not return again soon after the treatment. This is generally a longer process that requires effort from the patient.

Who is not willing to undertake this effort and, e.g. thinks that one could be healed without performing one's mandatory prayers on time, is wrong. He most probably will end up with a so-called healer, who takes large sums for a Ruqya session, but after some initial success everything will be as before. Or even with a sorcerer, who himself is working with Jinn, which in the end makes everything worse! On the contrary, the one who trusts in Allāh سبحانه و تعال and obeys Him, follows the advice of the Prophet ﷺ and does his part, will have success.

No disaster occurs without the permission of Allāh, including magic or the infestation with Jinn:

> *And from these two [angels] people learn that by which they cause division between man and wife; but they injure thereby no-one save by Allāh's leave. [Al-Baqarah 102]*

Every problem we have in life is a chance to improve, to make us stronger, to rely more on God and to fear Him more and to act better according to the Sunnah of the Prophet ﷺ. Who understands that Allāh سبحانه و تعالى never imposes a problem that can not be solved (unless it is already the beginning of a final punishment, may Allāh protect us) will inshaAllāh have patience because he realizes that Allāh has given him exactly this problem so that he can make progress and is led again to the right path.

Or think ye that ye will enter paradise while yet there hath not come unto you the like of [that which came to] those who passed away before you? Affliction and adversity befell them, they were shaken as with earthquake, till the messenger [of Allāh] and those who believed along with him said: When cometh Allāh's help? Now surely Allāh's help is nigh. [Al-Baqarah 214]

Every school kid knows that without examinations one can not get into a higher class and that one does not know one's position and where one still has shortages to correct.

Al-Bukhaari (6472) and Muslim (220) narrated from Ibn 'Abbaas (may Allāh be pleased with him) that the Messenger of Allāh (blessings and peace of Allāh be upon him) said: "Seventy thousand of my ummah will enter Paradise without being brought to account; they are the ones who did not ask for Ruqya or believe in omens or use cautery and they put their trust in their Lord."

These people will enter Paradise without being brought to account because of the perfection of their Tawheed, their complete trust in Allāh and their independence from people. The one who asks for Ruqya from others is not included in that seventy thousand who will enter Paradise without being brought to account, due to the shortfall in their trust in Allāh, because asking for Ruqya involves a kind of humiliation and need of the Raqi.

Muslim narrated (1043) that 'Awf ibn Maalik al-Ashja'i (may Allāh be pleased with him) said: We were with the Messenger of Allāh (blessings and peace of Allāh be upon him), nine or eight or seven (people) and he said: "Will you not swear allegiance to the Messenger of Allāh (blessings and peace of

Allāh be upon him)?" We had only recently sworn our allegiance, so we said: We have sworn our allegiance to you, O Messenger of Allāh. He said: "Will you not swear allegiance to the Messenger of Allāh (blessings and peace of Allāh be upon him)?' We said: We have already sworn our allegiance to you, O Messenger of Allāh. Then he said: "Will you not swear allegiance to the Messenger of Allāh (blessings and peace of Allāh be upon him)?" We held out our hands and said: We swear our allegiance to you, O Messenger of Allāh. Tell us on what basis we should swear allegiance to you? He said: "On the basis that you will worship Allāh and not associate anything with Him, and (you will perform) the five daily prayers, and you will obey Allāh – and he whispered – and you will not ask the people for anything." I saw that some of those people, if they dropped a whip, they would not ask anyone to hand it to them.

The perfection of the Tawheed is, among other things, not asking other people for anything, and it is precisely this perfection of Tawheed that is the best protection against Satan! A healer can only heal with the permission of Allāh, and without the help of the patient it is difficult, if not impossible, because the patient has to evade the Jinn everything the Jinn likes, such as sin and un-Islamic practices, and practice what Jinn do not like, Islam as eagerly as possible. That is why it makes no sense to search desperately for a healer, but one should immediately take action oneself, even before there is a problem. One should adhere to the commandments and prohibitions of Allāh and follow the Sunnah of the Prophet ﷺ, especially those Sunnahs which protect from the devils, and in case of possible infestations, carry out the procedures described in this book. If one is not able to do it by onself, one should keep in mind the listed criteria for a healer.

The book is intended to provide a first orientation to the novice Raqi and to serve as a reference, but hopefully the novice will have the opportunity to learn with an experienced Raqi.

Some people ask whether the techniques and treatment methods presented in this book were practiced by the Prophet ﷺ or the Salaf, may Allāh reward them for their taqwa! The answer is neither yes nor no. Basically, only methods based on Qur'an and Sunnah are presented, first of all the certainty that all healing is caused by Allāh alone, and that the Qur'an was sent down as a cure for the faithful but as a punishment for the criminals. Certain techniques are reported from the Prophet ﷺ, and based thereupon have God-fearing Raqis developed other techniques. Therefore one should perceive Ruqya less as "Islam" but more as "Islamic medicine".

> *Companions asked the Prophet ﷺ whether they should continue to practice Ruqya, as they did in the pre-Islamic period, on which the Prophet ﷺ replied: "Show me your methods. There is no harm in Ruqya as long as it does not contain shirk (polytheism)."* [1]

---

[1] Muslim

Jinn, Sihr

and ʿAin

The Jinn

The belief in the existence of Jinn is an integral part of Islam since the Qur'an speaks about the existence of man and Jinn. There is even a Sura called 'Al-Jinn'. Both humans and Jinn were created by Allāh سبحانه و تعال to serve and worship Him (Sura al-Dariyat 56).

Jinn are subtle beings living in the subtle world who normally have nothing to do with us. Like humans they have the ability to reflect and to choose freely (unlike angels and animals), that is why they are also responsible for their deeds.

The word "Jinn" in Arabic refers to something that is hidden and invisible. In this world the Jinn see us but we can not see them (in the hereafter, this is reversed), unless we are possessed by a Jinn or they take a visible form, sometimes as humans, but usually as black animals. (For the ordinary citizen, witches with black cats who sacrifice children to Satan, belong to the realm of fairy tales, just as sorcerers and all the strange beings like fairies and goblins.)

If the Jinn takes a visible form, it can not disappear as long as we look at it. This makes him extremely vulnerable, because when the Jinn come into our world, they can be easily fought (with God's word), as a shark can be fought on the mainland. Fear of the Jinn is therefore inappropriate. However, a precise definition of "their" and "our" world is not possible, since they can move and act in both. Both worlds are interwoven or parallel, so to speak. "Our world" is when they become visible or perceptible to us while "their world" is ghaib or where we can not see them (under normal circumstances).

The Messenger of Allāhs ﷺ said: "The Jinn are of three types: A type that has wings, and they fly through the air; a type that looks like snakes and dogs; and a type that stops for a rest then resumes its journey." [2]

There are believing Jinn and disbelievers. The vicious infidel Jinn are the Satans (Shaytan, majority Shayateen). A very bad Satan is called Maarid (Demon). If he is even worse, and at the same time strong, he is called Ifrit, and in the plural Afaart. The most powerful of all the Jinn is Iblis himself. He commands his troops like a general, and has army commanders.

Jabir bin Abdullah رضي الله عنه reported that the Prophet ﷺ said: "The throne of Iblis is on the sea and he sends out his troops to spread Fitna (evil, discord) among the people. The greatest (or best) of them, from his point of view, is the one that causes the most Fitna. One of the Satans would return after a mission and report to Iblis: "I have done this and that!" Iblis would answer, "You have not done anything!" So another would come and say, "I have not left this and that person without separating him from his wife." Iblis approaches this Satan and says to him, "How good you are!" [3]

The goal of Iblis is to lead as many people astray as possible so that they follow him to hell in the hereafter. He is our hereditary enemy, with whom there can be no peace. He hates us men because we were the cause of his condemnation. He was jealous of man and considered

---

[2] al-Tahhaawi in Mushkil al-Athaar, 4/95, al-Tabaraani in al-Kabir
[3] Muslim 17.157

himself something better, for which reason he did not want to bow before Adam:

> And when We said unto the angels: Fall down prostrate before Adam and they fell prostrate all save Iblis, he said: Shall I fall prostrate before that which Thou hast created of clay? He said: Seest Thou this [creature] whom Thou hast honoured above me, if Thou give me grace until the Day of Resurrection I verily will seize his seed, save but a few. He said: Go, and whosoever of them followeth thee - lo! Hell will be your payment, an ample payment. And excite any of them whom thou canst with thy voice, and urge thy horse and foot against them, and be a partner in their wealth and children, and promise them. Satan promiseth them only to deceive. Lo! My [faithful] bondmen - over them thou hast no power, and thy Lord sufficeth as [their] guardian. [Al-Isra '61-65]

> O Children of Adam! Let not Satan seduce you as he caused your [first] parents to go forth from the Garden and tore off from them their robe [of innocence] that he might manifest their shame to them. Lo! He seeth you, he and his tribe, from whence ye see him not. Lo! We have made the devils protecting friends for those who believe not. [Al-Araf 27]

> And when thou recitest the Qur'an, seek refuge in Allah from Satan the outcast. Lo! He hath no power over those who believe and put trust in their Lord. His power is only over those who make a friend of him, and those who ascribe partners unto Him [Allah]. [An-Nahl 98-100]

Allāh commands us to seek protection with Him so that Satan can not lead us astray.

He who follows Satan perceives his thoughts and deeds as good, reasonable and pleasing, but in the end he will always find that he has only followed delusion:

> And when Satan made their deeds seem fair to them and said: No-one of mankind can conquer you this day, for I am your protector. But when the armies came in sight of one another, he took flight, saying: Lo! I am guiltless of you. Lo! I see that which ye see not. Lo! I fear Allah. And Allah is severe in punishment. [Al-Anfal 48]

Satan was cursed for his arrogance, and this arrogance he tries to induce in man so that he thinks as Satan did: "I am better than him!" Whoever is arrogant follows Satan, and the Prophet ﷺ said that no one with a mustard seed of arrogance will enter paradise. Satan always tries to persuade us to assign partners to Allāh سبحانه و تعال, e.g. that we perform our deeds not for Allāh alone, but to obtain praise and prestige (Riya).

The Satan which leads us astray is actually not Iblis himself but one of his subordinates. Each person is accompanied by a Jinn called the Qarien, his personal Satan, which can not be expelled with Ruqya, because the Qarien is ordained by Allāh, and Allāh's will is not abrogated by Allāh's Word. This Qarien causes a person to do evil things and rebel against Allāh's law. On the last day, the person and his Qarien will lead a dispute before Allāh:

> His companion (the Qarien) says, "O our Lord, I did not seduce him to transgress, but he himself went astray." He said, "Do not dispute before Me, where

I had sent you the warning in advance. [Al-Qaf 26-27]

Abd-Allāh ibn Mas'ood رضي الله عنه reported that the Messenger of Allāh ﷺ said, "There is no one among you who has not assigned a companion of the Jinn." They asked, "Even to you, O Messenger of Allāh?" said, "Even to me, but Allāh has helped me with him, and he became a Muslim (or: I am secure of him), so he only asks me to do what is good." [4]

According to another report, "... He has assigned to him a companion of the Jinn and a companion of the angels."

In the Qur'an, ingratitude and unbelief are used synonymously. He who disbelieves, denies both Allāh as well as everything given by Allāh. Ingratitude often manifests itself in wastefulness:

Lo! The squanderers were ever brothers of the devils, and the devil was ever an ingrate to his Lord. [Al-Isra '27]

We may say that Satan and his band want to instigate exactly the opposite of what we call virtues. Faith in the One God, taqwa, humbleness, humility, honesty, loyalty, gratitude, right purpose, cleanliness, courage, modesty, shyness, selflessness, generosity, diligence, gentleness, sense of responsibility and so on. The more we realize these virtues and follow the Sunnah of the Prophet ﷺ, the more secure we are.

Disbelieving Jinn are dark, and the worse they become, the darker they become. On the other hand, faithful Jinn

---

[4] Muslim

are bright, and the more good they do, the more light they get until they are almost at the level of angels and can take orders from them, e.g. assisting believing humans.

There are male and female Jinn that can have offspring like humans. They do not marry. It is enough to love each other.

Jinn can also have sex with people, especially during dreams, and participate in the sexual intercourse of people if they forget to say "*Bismillah*" before it.

Jinn like to live in empty houses and on cemeteries, that's why indeed there can be a creepy atmosphere, which does not result of ghosts but in fact of "evil spirits". Are the evil Jinn in our homes, they evoke nightmares, especially in children.

In the house, Jinn prefer "quiet corners", where they are left alone, e.g. the attic. Believing Jinn often live in Muslim homes and protect the inhabitants against evil Jinn, but leave the house if the human inhabitants disobey God. Unfortunately, pious Jinn are rare. Like humans too, most of the Jinn are occupied with their daily lives and do not care much about religion.

Jinn also live in the forest, in the desert and on the sea, and find shelter in images of animated creatures, above all statues. The unbelieving Jinn do also like to stay on markets and shopping centers, where they cause mischief, and they love stench, which is why they are found in the toilet and generally in dirty places.

Jinn nourish themselves from old bones and food remnants (which should not be left over uncovered because this is almost an invitation for the Jinn, but should be covered with something while saying '*bismillah*').

Ibn Mas'ood رضي الله عنه said: The Messenger of Allāhs said: 'Someone from among the Jinn called me, and I went with him and recited Qur'an for them.' He took us and showed us the traces of where they had been and the traces of their fires. They asked him for food and he said, 'You can have every bone on which the name of Allah has been mentioned that comes into your possession, as meat, and all the droppings as food for your animals.' The Prophet said, 'So do not use [these things] for cleaning yourselves [after relieving oneself], for they are the food and provision of your brothers.'[5]

Jinn have different characters like humans. They have their own sects and groups, and there are Muslims, Jews, Christians, Catholics, Buddhists, Hindu, atheists and sun worshipers among them.

They have a simple life compared to mankind, since they do not produce anything, although they have the ability to do so, as we know from the Qur'an, where the Prophet Sulaiman عليه السلام used them to create palaces and many things. He also let them dive in the sea, which means that at least a group of them can live in the water.

Jinn feel more than they think, although they can memorize information quite well. But they do not process and link this information as humans do and therefore appear relatively dumb or uneducated. They have no books and do not go to school. They get their knowledge by listening to people or other Jinn. Many, however, have extensive experience because they are already very old, sometimes thousands of years.

---

[5] Reported by Muslim, 450

When a Jinn enters the body of a human being, he transmits his thoughts and feelings in a subtle form so that man interprets them as his own thoughts and feelings. Man begins to hate what the Jinn hates; to love what the Jinn loves; becomes angry when the Jinn becomes angry; is afraid if the Jinn is afraid, and so on.

In the same way that a Jinn imposes his thoughts and feelings upon the possessed man, a man can also force his thoughts and feelings upon the Jinn, and can overcome and dominate him. Every time the Jinn sends his negative thoughts or feelings, one counteracts by thinking the opposite and entertains positive thoughts. This weakens the Jinn considerably.

Jinn are made of pure, smokeless fire (but they are not fire), and cause a "hot temperament" in humans, which makes people lose control, which is why the Prophet ﷺ has always advised not to become angry. One knows the expressions like "hot anger", "burning envy" and so on. Smoke is their element, and any experienced Raqi will confirm that, without exception, all smokers are possessed by one or more Jinn, as well as all those who have any other kind of drug addiction. If Jinn remain in the body for an extended period of time, they typically cause diseases, both physical and mental. When they are in the body, they usually stay in the bloodstream, which is why they typically cause diseases that are related to blood.

The Prophet ﷺ said, "Shaytan flows through the son of Adam as the blood flows through his veins." [6]

All bad thoughts we entertain open the doors for attacks of Jinn. Every bad thought generates more evil

---

[6] Buchari 3.251

thoughts, and every evil deed generates evil deeds, as long as we do not remember God and repent, take another path and entertain other thoughts. That is why we have to gain control over our thoughts, especially by thinking of God.

> *And if a whisper from the devil reach thee then seek refuge in Allah. Lo! He is the Hearer, the Knower. [Fussilat 36]*

God-Rememberance (Dhikr) is the key to Ruqya and the ultimate weapon to be used against Satan and his band. The word "*Ruqya*" means "*seeking refuge*" or "*protecting*" or "*armed against sorcery*". And the best Dhikr and thus the best weapon and the best refuge is the reading of the Qur'an. In this way, we can not only overcome the whispering, but even destroy the Jinn.

> *And We reveal of the Qur'an that which is a healing and a mercy for believers though it increase the evil-doers in naught save ruin. [Al-Isra' 82]*

If someone makes good progress in Islam, Iblis will send him a special Satan, which is supposed to lead him astray. If the person has already brought his thoughts and emotions under control, and therefore is very difficult to be led astray, he is classified as dangerous by the Satans.

In all the cultures of the world, Jinn were and are being used for different purposes (see also the chapter "Jinn in other religions and cultures). In the case of "natural healers" such as shamans and medicine men, the "expulsion of evil spirits" is customary and is actually a win-win situation for all involved: the Jinn sent by the medicine man expels the Jinn who caused the disease and gets his sacrifice, the medicine man is paid by the patient, and the patient is cured. Everyone is happy! Too bad that this is all haram!

Sihr (magic)

Magic is a form of devil worship in which people bring Satan ritual sacrifices, so that the Jinn do "supernatural things" for them, primarily harm other people. Allāh promises people, who make use of the "services" of the Jinn, the hellfire [Al-Anam 128].

Magic can basically be used for almost anything, but it is usually used for:

- revenge

- harming someone who is envied

- acquiring illegitimate possession

- getting a desired woman (or a man)

- gaining power or success.

The sacrifices a sorcerer has to bring are usually signs of unbelief. He often has to do very humiliating and dirty things that we do not want to mention here. The greater the sacrifices, the greater the "services" the Satans perform for him. Animals, which are killed and thrown somewhere, are good enough for "normal jobs". Human sacrifices, especially those of children, are the summit of unbelief and the best "payment".

However, there are also forms of magic where there are no obvious forms of Satan worship and where Islam is even used as a camouflage. This is often found, e.g. in combat sports like Kung-Fu, Pencak Silat or self-defense techniques like Budi Suci, where one can also heal with hands. This type of "inner power" or "inner knowledge" (*ilmu batin*) also works with Jinn, but instead of obvious blasphemy, "*bid'ah*" (innovative practices) that oppose the Prophet's Sunnah is used instead.

In other religions, Satan worship is more subtle. In the appendix one will find a chapter dealing with this topic (Jinn in other religions and cultures).

Either the sorcerer uses a Jinn to whom he assigns a job, or he uses magic poison, or both, e.g. the Jinn infuses the poison into the body of the victim. Objects can also be bewitched, e.g. a car with which one always has breakdowns or even accidents; or a business which nose dives or where endless quarrels break out.

The most popular forms of Sihr are briefly presented here.

Sihr Tafriq

This magic is used to divide people and make them quarrel. In the Qur'an, the relationship between husband and wife is specifically mentioned, but magic can strain or even destroy any relationship.

Sihr Mahabbah

This magic is used to arouse "love" for someone and make the victim submissive.

Sihr Khumul / Junuun

With this magic the victim is driven mad. The Jinn attacks the brain.

Sihr Hawatif

This magic is used to instil a whisper in the mind, either to just mislead the victim or to motivate it to do something, maybe even to commit suicide (see incident in Düsseldorf in the preface).

Sihr Jilb at-Tahyil

This magic is similar to Sihr Mahabbah. The victim is brought to the house of the magician and abused.

Sihr Ta'til az-Zawwaaj

This magic is used to prevent someone from entering into a relationship with someone else, e.g. to marry. Either one suddenly sees the future partner in a very negative light, so that one no longer wants to marry him, or something always prevents the marriage.

Sihr Maridh

This magic is used to make someone sick. It can cause almost any disease. The Jinn usually goes into the brain and damages the corresponding nerves.

Sihr Nadzif

This magic extends the period of the woman's monthly bleeding so that the woman is constantly bleeding, which can lead to premature birth.

Sihr Rabth

This magic is aimed at the sexual organs of the spouses, so that their love life is so disturbed that it often comes to divorce.

Sihr Adamul Injab

This magic is used so that the woman or the man can not get any children, as the Jews threatened they would do with the Muhajirien so that they would not get any offspring.

Sorcery often manifests itself in dreams, where, for example, one is bitten, falls from large heights or is injured. Often one even sees the person who hurts one.

Different types of transmission

We can divide the transmission paths of magic into four types: eaten, stepped upon, placed in the body and done over distance.

Eaten Magic will in 95% of the cases cause digestive problems: gastric or intestinal troubles may accompany nausea and vomiting. These difficulties are usually permanent, sometimes they only exist for a short time and then disappear.

If a person suffers from these stomach problems and has other symptoms as described above, he can be almost certain that he is a victim of eaten magic.

Stepped upon Magic is often accidental: it was there for some reason, and one stepped on it. It mainly affects the skin: wounds, eczema (also psoriasis) and pressure points on the body and usually on the legs; sometimes at changing places and medically unexplained. It can also cause hair to fall or to cause weakness in the legs.

The magic will have only these physical effects for someone for whom it was not intended. It is usually placed in front of the victim's house. If the targeted victim steppes upon this magic, it unfolds its full effect and generates not only skin problems, but also other problems of all kinds.

Magic placed into the body is implanted by Jinn. The sorcerer uses them to send the magic to the spot where it is to cause pain and dysfunction. For example, in a woman, the magic is placed in the ovaries, so that she can not get children, or into the man's testicles, so that he becomes impotent. Or the magic simply prevents the Jinn who was sent to get expelled again. As long as one does not treat the magic together with the Jinn, the Ruqya will be ineffective.

Magic over distance is the most classic and most common type of sorcery. Depending on where the Buhul[7] is hidden, it has different effects:

➢ If it is hung in a high place, it will dominate and envelop the person, and whatever the person is doing, he only turns in circles and returns to the same point again and again. Or he lives in a detached, imaginary world, with doubts, anxiety, indecisiveness or change in mood. It can also cause severe headaches or make him dream, he rises to high places or fall from big heights.

➢ Buried in the earth, it sucks the power and the energy from a person, causing uneasy sleep and giving the person a depressed look and the mentality of a loser.

➢ Buried in a graveyard, the person becomes "like dead", apathetic and depressed. He no longer sees a future, lives day by day, thinks a lot about death and dreams of dead people or graves.

➢ If the magic is hidden in a well, the victim "remains at the bottom of the well" symbolically speaking, e.g. financially, and will never come out.

➢ Magic with a chain or padlock: the person will be chained, e.g. his business gets blocked. It can also chain Jinn to the person.

➢ Knots are often used to block communication: As soon as one begins to discuss, one quarrels. Or obstacles appear, and every time one has overcome an obstacle the next appears. Or "knots" in thinking: thinking always stops at fixed points.

---

[7] The thing on which the magic is tied. I am using here the Indonesian name and not Ta'wies because there is difference of opinion about Ta'wies. Please see the article in the appendix: "Are Ta'wies allowed?"

> Dolls are used by placing needles in them, which then cause stitches in the body of the person or cause diseases. The doll can also be burnt, cut, buried, etc.

> All sorts of other magic of which the sorcerers always invent new ones: using tar to make the person appear dark, so that people avoid him; using fat to make the person fat; donkey ears to make him dumb; dog hair, so that it becomes mean and aggressive; frogs, so that it becomes repugnant and so on.

The above magic can be endlessly combined. If it is not treated, it remains a lifetime. When different types of magic are sent, the effects add up. Someone really ill-wishing can send so much magic that the victim soon loses control of himself and his life.

There is also serial magic: each time a magic has been successfully treated, the next one will automatically begin to work.

'Ain (evil eye)

A person looks at another envious, whereupon the other person is "broken", e.g. an industrious student suddenly becomes lazy, or a successful athlete doesn't win anymore. Children, and especially "sweet" babies, are often hit by 'Ain. Even things like car, business, house and other things can be hit.

'Ain can have both physical and psychological negative effects similar to those of magic and infestation by Jinn.

Causes of attack by Jinn

Shall I inform you upon whom the devils descend? They descend on every sinful, false one. [As-Suara 221-222]

And he whose sight is dim to the remembrance of the Beneficent, We assign unto him a devil who becometh his comrade; And lo! they surely turn them from the way of Allah, and yet they deem that they are rightly guided. [Az-Zukhruf 36-37]

Commonly, a religious life with regular prayer, Qur'an reading and adhering to essential Sunnah protects against the attack of Jinn. But in many cases this is not sufficient, for the causes of the attack of Jinn are many:

➤ Black magic

➤ 'Ain, "evil eye"

➤ Sin of all kinds. The graver the sin, the more the doors are open and the more Jinn can enter.

➤ Inheritance: An ancestor has made a pact with Jinn and allowed him and his descendants to occupy the body of subsequent generations.

➤ Learning of certain combat techniques that can make invulnerable or be able to beat opponents over distances, as often the case with Pencak Silat or Kung-Fu.

➤ Jinn fall in love with a human or abuse him sexually.

➤ One accidentally injures a Jinn and he takes revenge, or e.g. one has unknowingly cut the tree on which he lived.

➢ In general, a human offers Jinn a home, where he has food and accommodation, usually better than he can find it elsewhere.

Often there is no obvious reason or occasion, but in general it needs an occasion and a "gap", so that the Jinn can enter. If the defenses of man are not active, which on the spiritual plane are faith, God-remembrance and adherence to the Sunnah of the Prophet ﷺ, and especially when man becomes emotional (very angry, sad or anxious), he is vulnerable.

It is not surprising in today's conditions that the infestation by Jinn has become epidemic. The further the infestation has advanced, the more difficult the cure becomes; not because the healing is difficult in itself, but because the person concerned is so subjugated by Satan that he himself does not want any healing and feels a strong antipathy towards the healing process and potential healers. Thus, e.g. the person concerned is not able to read the Qur'an or does not want to visit a Raqi. And it is nearly impossible to help someone who does not want to be helped.

Sadly, there is an enormous ignorance about Ruqya and symptoms are often not recognized, although healing would be simple in most cases: the mere reading of certain verses of the Qur'an with appropriate intention. Something that every Muslim should be able to do!

Symptoms of infestation by Jinn or Sihr

Here are a few possible symptoms listed that may occur individually or in combination. If someone has several of these symptoms or a significant one (e.g. one can see Jinn), one should immediately try self-healing, and if one does not feel any relief after sufficient efforts one should go to a healer.

➢ Uncontrolled emotions, especially anger or grief

➢ Frequently doubt, pondering and anxiety, without any apparent reason

➢ Difficulties to concentrate during prayer and often forgetting the number of Rakaat.

➢ Difficulties to breathe or heavy tiredness while reading the Qur'an

➢ Absence of mind, living in a fantasy world, or one likes to segregate oneself

➢ A weak state of mind and the feeling of mental pressure

➢ Unexplained pain such as headache, toothache, pain in the chest, throat, stomach, etc., especially if they reoccur at certain times, e.g. always at 9 am or always before prayer

➢ Depression

➢ Cardiac dysfunction or severe heart palpitations

➢ Lazy to worship, disregard of the Sunnah, but swift to sin

➢ Chronic fatigue

➢ Chronic nausea and / or chronic revulsion

- Epileptic spasms or otherwise losing consciousness
- Hearing voices
- Hearing problems (tinnitus, sudden hearing loss)
- Paranoid conditions and inexplicable fears
- One often smells incense or other strange fragrances, also the smell of carrion or rotten things
- Dizziness, or one sees objects moving
- Strange deeds or movements that one would not otherwise do as if hanging on a strip
- Supernatural skills, such as fortune telling, reading other people's thoughts, or often Déjà-vu
- The feeling or perception of a "presence" or a being. Somebody is behind one, watching one, follows one or touches one
- Diseases for which no doctor can find an explanation
- Poor sleep, frequent waking up
- Difficulties to wake up, especially to prayer
- Something keeps one firm in one's sleep or presses on one, and it takes a great effort to get rid of it and wake up
- Dreams in which one is very troubled and want to call for help but is not able to
- One sees strange, scary things in the dream
- One is often dreaming of certain animals such as cats, dogs, camels, snakes, foxes, mice, etc.
- Frequently crying, laughing, screaming, grinding teeth, etc. during sleep

- One dreams of falling from great heights
- One often dreams of death or graves
- One always meets the same people in a dream
- One sees in the dream indistinct beings
- Dream that comes true the next day
- Sleepwalking
- Impotence
- Infertility
- Strong pain during menstruation or uterine problems
- High cholesterol or sugar levels
- Cramps, especially at night
- "Dirty Thoughts"
- Uncontrolled sex drive or masturbation
- One often has sex in a dream or is even raped
- Homosexuality
- Bipolar
- Difficulties finding a spouse, or one finds one, but always something prevents the marriage
- Often dispute with the spouse, divorce
- Constant quarreling
- Turning around in life, nothing succeeds
- One sees crosses during prayer, doubts about Allāh and predetermination, etc.
- Stroke

- Hypertension, heart diseases of all kinds, pulmonary diseases
- One often feels prickling at different body parts, especially the shoulder
- Eczema and especially psoriasis
- Very naughty child, hyperactive, quickly gets angry, does not want to learn, pray, etc.
- Quickly exhausted, difficult breathing, chest pain
- The house appears dark and frightening
- Frequently nausea
- Frequent belching and burping
- Permanent postponement of important things
- Hatred towards other people, family, friends
- Business bankruptcy
- One loses money all the time
- Losing work or rank
- One is afraid to look into the mirror
- Face often pale or yellowish
- Body often feels hot
- Constant yawning
- Loss of appetite
- General laziness
- Not being able to concentrate
- Joking and laughing in excess
- Feeling of numbness in different body parts

➤ Cold feeling in different body parts

➤ Generally: abnormalities and excesses, for which there is no apparent cause

If one is worried about being affected, one should take precaution and treat it and do not delay it for any reason. Ruqya has no negative side effects, and it is not intended solely for the expulsion of Jinn, but also an alternative healing method. A companion of the Prophet ﷺ for example healed the sting of a scorpion with the help of Surat al-Fatihah.

Basic safety measures

The measures to protect oneself against Jinn, Magic and 'Ain are corresponding with those one should take if a problem has already occurred.

Tawheed. There is no greater protection from the trials of this world and the next than to confirm by knowing and acting that Allāh is alone in His reign, in our worship of Him, and in His perfect names and attributes.

He is the master of everything, the owner, creator and provider. He is the one who gives life and death. He is the one who causes benefits and harm. He is the only one who can respond in time of an emergency. He is the one who has control over everything, and all the good is in His hand. He is the one who does everything by His will and His commandment. He knows everything and can do anything. He is Al-Qayyūm (the maintainer of all) who is not overwhelmed by slumber nor sleeps. He has a will that is always executed, and wisdom that is infinite. And He is all-hearing, all-seeing, kind and merciful. To Him alone we pray, with pure devotion; with love, fear, hope, trust, longing and awe. Not a bit of our worship is to be made for anyone but Him.

When we confirm this and act accordingly, we are protected by the promise of Allāh سبحانه و تعالى, who said:

Those who believe and obscure not their belief by wrongdoing, theirs is safety; and they are rightly guided. [Al-Anam 82]

The Prophet ﷺ explained that the wrongdoing mentioned here is to add to Allāh سبحانه و تعالى something in devotion and worship. The greatest protection is therefore in Tawheed. And whoever does not have Tawheed will find no protection but is lost:

> *Turning unto Allah [only], not ascribing partners unto Him; for whoso ascribeth partners unto Allah, it is as if he had fallen from the sky and the birds had snatched him or the wind had blown him to a far-off place. [Al-Hajj 31]*

Sunnah. The struggle to follow the Sunnah of the Prophet ﷺ is another reason for protection, without which other forms of protection will have no effect. Allāh says:

> *Then let those beware who withstand the Messenger's order, lest some trial befall them, or a grievous penalty be inflicted on them. [An-Nur 63]*

Allāh gives no protection to the one who opposes the commandments of the Prophet ﷺ, but on the contrary, he threatens him punishment.

> *If anyone contends with the Messenger even after guidance has been plainly conveyed to him, and follows a path other than that becoming to men of Faith, We shall leave him in the path he has chosen, and land him in Hell,- what an evil refuge! [An-Nisa 115]*

Important Sunnahs associated with Jinn are e.g.: not yawning with open mouth; not eating or drinking while standing or with left hand; travelling in community; avoiding being outside the house between the Maghrib and Isha prayer (especially important for children); lowering one's gaze before the other sex; avoiding "bad places" (for example, not staying longer in the market or the toilet as absolutely necessary); following the etiquettes of sleeping (see appendix) and so on.

The obligatory prayer. The Prophet ﷺ said that the difference between a Muslim and a non-Muslim would be the prayer, and whoever omits it intentionally would be disbelieving. Such a person does not deserve the protection of Allāh, and Allāh سبحانه و تعالى has promised him hell (Al-Maun 4-5). One should make it as punctual as possible.

Taqwa. In a practical sense, fearing God means doing as many good deeds as one can with the right intention and in accordance with the Sunnah of the Prophet ﷺ, and comitting as little sins as possible. Taqwa is the most frequent advice in the Qur'ân, and there is no doubt that every good deed done is a source of protection, while every sin is a possible cause of harm:

> When a single disaster smites you, although ye smote [your enemies] with one twice as great, do ye say? - "Whence is this?" Say [to them]: "It is from yourselves: For Allah hath power over all things." [Ali Imran 165]

> Mischief has appeared on land and sea because of [the meed] that the hands of men have earned, that [Allah] may give them a taste of some of their deeds: in order that they may turn back [from Evil]. [Ar-Rum 41]

Du'a and Dhikr. One should seek the protection of Allāh through Du'a (Invocation) and through recommended Dhikr (God-Remembrance). This must be done regularly and habitually, and not just for one day. It is also necessary that the heart is engaged together with the tongue, so you understand the meaning of the prayer, and that the person acts in accordance with the Du'a being done. This is the most perfect form of the remembrance of Allāh.

The best form of recollection of Allāh is the recitation of the Qur'ân, it contains protection from every evil. Allāh سبحانه و تعالى says:

> *When thou dost recite the Qur'an, We put, between thee and those who believe not in the Hereafter, a veil invisible. [Al-Isra' 45]*

The Prophet ﷺ told us that sorcerers are not able to act against the recitation of Sura al-Baqarah, and he told us that the recitation of the last two verses of al-Baqarah at night suffices a person. He also told us about the effect of the last two Suras of the Qur'an, al-Falaq and an-Nas as well as Sura al-Ikhlas. All these Suras and the general recitation of the Qur'an are a protection.

Protection of the house, as a means for protection of oneself. The house should be a fortress that repels the Satans. A house inviting the Satans is one in which people are not protected. Since e.g. angels enter no house, where there is a dog or a picture, the probability is very high that the house is instead entered by Satans.

The house - or the room, if the person does not have control over the whole house - should be cleansed of anything that could attract the Satans, e.g. pictures (of living creatures), inadequate movies, music, dirt and stench, including cigarettes. It should be a place of prayer, a place of learning of Islam and a place of obedience to Allāh. One should keep the windows and doors closed between Maghrib and Isha prayers, and also as much as possible during the night. One should read Sura al-Baqarah and the recommended Adhkaar. One should spray the house once a month from inside and outside with a Ruqya water (see the chapter "Variant of the Ruqya bath and cleaning the house of Jinn or magic")

Recitation of important Adhkaar. The following verses and Dhikr formulas are the most important ones that should be memorized and practiced regularly. One has to learn the following, with Arabic pronunciation. The correct pronunciation of the below-mentioned Suras as an audio file should be easily found on the Internet.

Bismillah - In the Name of Allāh

It is best to say it before each activity, but always when entering and leaving the house; before the meal (since Satan can not find accommodation or food if recited), before entering the toilet; before taking off the clothes and before sexual intercourse.

Al-Fatitah – The Opening

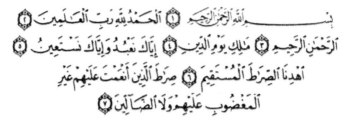

Bismillah-hir-rahman nir rahiem. Al-hamdulillah-hir-rabbil a'lameen, ar-rahman nir-raheem, maliki yaumid-deen. Iyyaka na' budu' wa iyyaka nasta'in. Ihdinas-sirathal mustaqeem, sirathal-lasina an amta alaihim, ghairil maghduubi alaihim wa lad-dhaalleen.

In the name of Allah, the Beneficent, the Merciful. Praise be to Allah, Lord of the Worlds, The Beneficent, the Merciful, Master of the Day of Judgment, Thee [alone] we worship; Thee [alone] we ask for help. Show us the straight path, the path of those whom Thou hast favoured; Not the [path] of those who earn Thine anger nor of those who go astray.

Whenever one reads Qur'an, one should read this Sura first. It is said that this Sura contains the whole Qur'an. Must be recited at every Shalat and is part of every Ruqya.

Al-Ikhlas – Purity of Faith

Qul huwal-lahu ahad, al-lahus-samad, lam yalid wa lamyuulad, wa lam yakul-lahu kufu-wan ahad.

Say: He is Allah, the One and Only; Allah, the Eternal, Absolute; He begetteth not, nor is He begotten; and there is none like unto Him.

Al-Falaq – The dawn

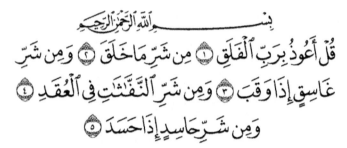

Qul a'usu birabbil falaq, min scharri maa chalaq, wa min scharri ghaasiqin isa waqab, wa min scharrin-naffaasaati fil 'uqad wa min sharri hasideen isa hasad.

Say: I seek refuge in the Lord of the Daybreak; from the evil of that which He created; from the evil of the darkness when it is intense, and from he evil of malignant witchcraft, and from the evil of the envier when he envieth.

An-Naas – Mankind

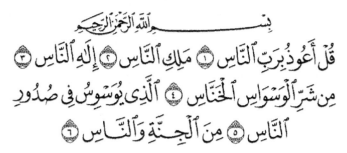

Qul 'ausubirabbin-naas, malikin-naas, ilaahin-naas, min sharril waswaasil channaas, allasi yuwaswisu fie shuduurin-naas, minal Jinnati wan-naas.

Say: I seek refuge with the Lord and Cherisher of Mankind, The King of Mankind, The god [or judge] of Mankind, from the mischief of the Whisperer [of Evil], who withdraws [after his whisper], [The same] who whispers into the hearts of Mankind, Among Jinn and among men.

The three Suras above (al-Ikhlas, al-Falaq and An-Naas) should be recited three times in the morning (after the Fajr prayer) and three times in the afternoon (after the 'Asr prayer). They will suffice against every single thing.

Before leaving the house it is good practice to recite them three times, blow in the hands and rub the body (and those of the children).

Al-Baqarah 255 – Ayat-ul-kursi

اللَّهُ لَا إِلَٰهَ إِلَّا هُوَ
الْحَيُّ الْقَيُّومُ لَا تَأْخُذُهُ سِنَةٌ وَلَا نَوْمٌ لَّهُ مَا فِي السَّمَاوَاتِ
وَمَا فِي الْأَرْضِ مَن ذَا الَّذِي يَشْفَعُ عِندَهُ إِلَّا بِإِذْنِهِ يَعْلَمُ
مَا بَيْنَ أَيْدِيهِمْ وَمَا خَلْفَهُمْ وَلَا يُحِيطُونَ بِشَيْءٍ مِّنْ عِلْمِهِ إِلَّا
بِمَا شَاءَ وَسِعَ كُرْسِيُّهُ السَّمَاوَاتِ وَالْأَرْضَ وَلَا يَئُودُهُ حِفْظُهُمَا
وَهُوَ الْعَلِيُّ الْعَظِيمُ ﴿٢٥٥﴾

Allāhu – la ilaaha illa huwal hayyul qayyuum, la ta'chusuhu sinatuw-wa la naum, lahu maa fis-samawaati wa maa fil ardh, man salasi yaschfa'u 'indahu illa bi isni, ya'lamu maa baina aidihim wa maa chalfahum, wa la yuhiethuuna bi shaim-min 'ilmihi illa bimaa shaa-a, wa si'a kursiyuhus-samawaati wal ardh, wa la ya uduhu hifsahuma, wa huwal 'aliyul 'athiem.

Allah! There is no god but He,- the Living, the Self-subsisting, Eternal. No slumber can seize Him nor sleep. His are all things in the heavens and on earth. Who is there can intercede in His presence except as He permitteth? He knoweth what [appeareth to His creatures as] before or after or behind them. Nor shall they compass aught of His knowledge except as He willeth. His Throne doth extend over the heavens and the earth, and He feeleth no fatigue in guarding and preserving them for He is the Most High, the Supreme [in glory].

An especially important verse for Ruqya and the most powerful. Very good to be recited after every obligatory prayer (there is nothing between you and paradise except death) and before one goes to sleep. (Allāh سبحانه و تعالى will send a protector to shield you against anything, and Satan will not approach you.) Seven times after each compulsory prayer, protects inshaAllāh against most attacks, including sorcery.

The Du'a for entering the toilet:

اللَّهُمَّ إِنِّي أَعُوذُ بِكَ مِنَ الْخُبُثِ وَالْخَبَائِثِ

Bismillaah, Allāhumma inni a'uudhu bika minal-khubuthi wal-khabaa'ith.

O Allāh, I seek refuge with you from all evil and evil-doers. [8]

One is protected from the male and female Satans who are in the bathroom.

The Du'a for leaving the house:

بِسْمِ اللهِ ، تَوَكَّلْتُ عَلَى اللهِ

وَلَا حَوْلَ وَلَا قُوَّةَ إِلَّا بِاللهِ

Bismillaahi, tawakkaltu 'alal-laahi, wa laa haula wa laa quata illaa billaah.

In the name of Allāh, I place my trust in Allah and there is no might nor power except with Allāh. [9]

The angels say, "You will be defended, protected, and guided," and you will be protected from Satan (as long as one does not commit sins, then the angels leave and the Satans will return.)

---

[8] Muslim 375
[9] Abu Dawud 5095

The Du'a for setting foot in a new place

(like getting out oft he car, entering a house, when sitting somewhere outside etc.)

أَعُوذُ بِكَلِمَاتِ اللهِ التَّامَّاتِ مِنْ شَرِّ مَا خَلَقَ

A'udhu bi kalimaat-illaahit-taammaati min sharri maa khalaq.

I seek refuge in Allāh's perfect words from the evil which He has created.[10]

Nothing will hurt one until one leaves the place.

The following supplication,

which should get recited three times in the morning (after Fajr) and three times in the afternoon (after 'Asr):

بِسْمِ اللهِ الَّذِي لَا يَضُرُّ مَعَ اسْمِهِ شَيْءٌ فِي الْأَرْضِ
وَلَا فِي السَّمَاءِ وَهُوَ السَّمِيعُ الْعَلِيمُ (ثَلَاثُ مَرَّاتٍ)

Bismillaahil-ladhi laa yaḍurru ma'asmihi shay'un fil-arḍi wa laa fis-samaa'i wa huwas-sami'-ul-'alim.

In the name of Allah, by whose name nothing can cause harm neither on earth nor in the heaven and He is The All-Hearing, The All-Knowing.[11]

Nothing shall harm you for the rest of the day / night.

---

[10] Muslim 2708; At-Tirmidhi 3437; Ibn Majah 3547
[11] Abu Dawood 5088; At-Tirmidhi 3388; Ibn Majah 3869

And the following dhikr[12],

which should get recited ten times in the morning (after Fajr) and ten times in the afternoon (after 'Asr), the best is 100-times a day:

$$\text{لَا إِلَهَ إِلَّا اللّٰهُ ، وَحْدَهُ لَا شَرِيكَ لَهُ ، لَهُ الْمُلْكُ وَلَهُ الْحَمْدُ ، يُحْيِي وَيُمِيتُ ، وَهُوَ عَلَى كُلِّ شَيْءٍ قَدِيرٌ}$$

Laa ilaaha ill-Allāhu, waḥdahu laa sharika lahu, lahul-mulku wa lahul-ḥamdu, yuḥyi wa yumitu, wa huwa 'alaa kulli shay'in qadir.

There is no (true) god except Allah, alone and without any partners. To Him belongs the dominion, He deserves all praise. He gives life and death, and He is capable of everything.

Allāh سبحانه و تعالى will send angels to protect one from Satan until the morning / evening comes. One will also receive ten rewards and ten sins will be forgiven. And when one says it 100 times a day, no one has better deeds than the one who says it more often.

Other protective measures:

➢ One should pronounce the name of Allāh whenever one becomes emotional (angry, sad or anxious). When one is angry, one should sit down, if one is already sitting, one should lie down.

➢ In order to prevent the evil eye, every time one admires something, one should pronounce the name of Allāh: "MashaAllāh" ("What Allah willth"), "TabarakAllāh" ("Allāh is blessed"), etc. One should say it also for others if they forget it.

_____

[12] At-Tirmidhi 3534 and 3553

- One should not show one's possessions and abilities in order to prevent envy, because this can lead to 'Ain or even bewitching.

- Ibn 'Abbas رضي الله عنه said: "The Prophet ﷺ sought refuge for Hasan and Husayn, saying: '*Your father (with whom he meant the prophet Ibrahim عليه السلام) sought refuge with Allāh for Isma'il and Ishaq with these words: A`udhu bi kalimat Allāh al-tammah min kulli shaytanin wa hammah wa min kulli `aynin lammah (I seek refuge in Allāh's perfect words of every Satan and poisonous reptile, and of every evil eye).'*"

- Never give any personal belongings to suspicious strangers or allow them to take photos. Very careful with obtrusive and individually offered food, or when unusual presents are made!

- One should read Sura al-Baqarah at least once a month in one's house.

- Every time one feels that something is attacking or harassing, one should immediately perform additional worship. For example, when one has bad dreams at night, best to get up for Tahajjud prayer. When Satan sees that one is always reacting in this way, his enthusiasm to annoy one, is considerably slowed down inshaAllāh.

- Personal hygiene is very important: cutting of fingernails weekly, shaving of armpit and pubic hair, often brushing of teeth (possibly with miswak), etc.

- One should always be in the state of ritual purity (ablution).

- And the first and last, and although we repeat it again and again, one should fear Allāh سبحانه و تعال (by observing his commandments and prohibitions), beseeching his protection, never giving up one's hope in Allāh, but exercising patience in every trial, which Allāh imposes on one. InshaAllāh it will be then the best for one. And, of course, as often as possible, remembering Allāh سبحانه و تعال in fear and gratitude:

If a suggestion from Satan assail thy [mind], seek refuge with Allah; for He heareth and knoweth [all things]. Those who fear Allah, when a thought of evil from Satan assaults them, bring Allah to remembrance, when lo! they see [aright]! [Al-Araf 200-201]

What one should not use for protection

One should never use the help of magicians, "shamans" or practices of other religions, such as placing nails in the corner of each room or scattering chilli powder on the floor. All this is forbidden and removes the protection of Allāh سبحانه و تعالى, because either one joins something with Allāh (commits Shirk) or does not follow the Sunnah of the Prophet ﷺ.

Whether it is permitted to use a Ta'wies, see the article "Are Ta'wies Allowed?" in the appendix.

Self-Treatment

In general, Jinn can hide behind unbelief and sins like behind a wall. Many Raqis therefore refuse to treat people who have not yet made Taubat (repentance). In fact, it makes little sense to carry out the following treatments if one does not want to correct one's mistakes.

It may be that there is no negligence on one's own behalf, especially in case of Magic or 'Ain. Nevertheless, it should be a reason to intensify worship. The protective measures mentioned in the previous chapter should therefore be the minimum that the patient does on his own initiative, apart from the treatment as such.

'Ain is the thing which commonly can be treated most easily: Take the water used for *wudhu* and *ghusl* (best from the one who has cast the evil eye, which of course will not be possible in most cases), and pour it over the patient.

If one does not feel any improvement, and also in cases of other complaints, like attacks by Jinn and magic / witchcraft, then one should follow the 7-day program.

7-day detoxification program

This program is recommended by Shaykh 'Adil ibn Ṭahir al-Muqbil for all those who complain about problems related to Jinn, magic, and the evil eye. The Shaykh said he has been using it with great success for many years, and it is especially important for those who have not yet found a healer (Raqi). The Shaykh calls it "The Collection of Cures" because it consists of a series of things that are mentioned in Qur'an and Sunnah as a healing (Shifaa).

Since the program is not cited as a whole in the Sunnah, it is not necessary to carry out each part without modification. Thus, when e.g. a diabetic can not eat honey, he can omit it, although it is nevertheless recommended to make the program the same as mentioned.

Before beginning:

1. One should humble oneself before Allāh سبحانه و تعالى.

2. One should make du'a at the times when du'a is best accepted as between the Adzan and the Iqamah, the last third of the night, between the Asr prayer and the Maghrib prayer, the two sermons on Friday, during rain etc.

The following things should be kept ready:

Water - (about 3-5 liters per person) - preferably Zam-Zam water, because of the hadith: *"A food that satisfies and a cure from sickness"* and *"The water of Zam Zam is for whatever it is drunk for."* If Zam-Zam is not available, rainwater should be gathered, for Allāh said, *"And We have sent down blessed rain from the sky and made grow thereby gardens and grain from the harvest"* [Qaf 9], and because the Prophet ﷺ used to uncover part of his garment when it rained, and he would say, *"It has just come from its Lord.[13]"* If rain water is not available, then regular water is fine, but effort should be made to obtain rain water where Zam Zam is not available. {Please do not delay the program excessively waiting for Zam Zam or rain water - you can always add it later inshaAllāh.)

Olive oil - One bottle per person should be enough. This should be organic extra virgin olive oil - greenish in color, not yellow as vegetable oil. Recommended is organic extra virgin olive oil from Palestine when you can get it because

---

[13] Abu Dawood

it comes from a country that is blessed. This is because Allah describes it as *"lit from a blessed tree - the olive"* [An-Nur 35], and the Prophet ﷺ said, *"Eat olive oil and oil yourselves with it, for it is from a blessed tree.[14]"*

Honey - which should be organic and of good quality. Allāh تعالى و سبحانه said, *"From their bodies comes a drink, many in color"* [An-Nahl 69] and the Prophet ﷺ said, *"There is a cure in three things, a drunk of honey ...[15]"* The Sheikh stressed that many people make the mistake to eat the honey and not to drink it, but the hadith makes it clear that one should drink the honey diluted in water.

Black Seeds (Nigella sativa) - again this should be organic. The Prophet ﷺ said, *"It is a cure for every disease.[16]"*

Sidr (Ziziphus) leaves[17] - is not listed by Shaykh Muqbil in this program. However, we strongly recommend it, since we have already often witnessed its effects. Seven leaves are crushed and put into the water to be recited on.

At the beginning of the week one has to sit and put the water and the olive oil in front of oneself. Then one recites the following:

1. (A) **al-Fatihah** (Suras and verses, see appendix) - seven times is best, or three times, if one wishes, because the Prophet ﷺ has approved this. (B) **al-Baqarah** - once all through (If one is not able to read al-Baqarah, then read what is easy for you, or ask someone to read for you if you struggle to read the Qur'an). (C) **The last three Suras** of the

---

[14] Tirmidhi
[15] Buchari
[16] Bukhari and Muslim
[17] http://sunnahfoods.co.uk/product/sidr-leaves

Qur'an: al-Ikhlas, al-Falaq and an-Nas - three times each. (D) **Ayat-ul-Kursi** (al-Baqara 255) - seven times is best, or three times, if one wishes.

2. Blow on the water and the olive oil (as though you are spitting but without spittle), either after every verse or Sura, or what is easy for you. When the entire reading is finished, you can start the program. (In the same way water is prepared to e.g. spray the house.)

On the first three days:

1. Two tablespoons of honey are dissolved in a cup of the water that you have read upon. Add seven seeds of black seed and drink. Do this three times a day.

2. Before sleeping, anoint the entire body from head to toe with the read-on olive oil.

3. In the morning, wash the whole body with soap and water. Take half a cup of the read-on water and put in a bucket or other container. Then fill the bucket with water from the water tap and wash the whole body.

On the fourth to seventh day:

1. With the read-on olive oil anoint any aching or painful areas.

2. Two tablespoons of honey are dissolved in a cup of the read-on water. Add seven seeds of black seed and drink it. Do this three times a day.

What to expect:

1. On the first day one will most probably not feel anything.

2. On the second and third day one feels very sick. One can feel excessive fatigue, pain all over the body or

pain at certain places, sometimes as if one has done a strenuous exercise.

3. On the fourth day one feels completely refreshed, as if one has a lot of energy - with the permission of Allāh.

4. The pain will gradually disappear in the course of the seven days, inshaAllāh.

5. If the patient does not feel better or the 7-day program results in a worsening of the symptoms, then it is advised to move on to the full Ruqya program, where the 7-day program is repeated 1-2 times a month, in addition to other Ruqya.

NOTE: There is no reason why one can not implement this program in Ramadan. Just drink the mixture at Maghrib, after the Tarawiḥ and before the Fajr prayer. Also for a menstruating woman the program is possible.

Full Ruqya program

If the problem is more serious and the 7-day program has not helped, one should make the full program, which requires a strict minimum program, either solely by self-treatment or, if necessary, with the help of friends and family members.

It is also recommended that patients or their family and friends make a record of how much they do every day, and record any changes, so in case a Raqi is consulted, he is well informed and can choose the best form of treatment, should there be no improvement despite one's own efforts.

Preconditions for treatment:

❖ That the patient worships Allāh سبحانه و تعالى alone, trusts in Allāh alone, and recognizes that there is no healing except from Allāh.

❖ That the patient follows the Sunnah of the Messenger of Allāh ﷺ as good as possible and does not practice something that opposes it.

❖ That the patient is not in possession of an amulet and the like.

❖ That the patient's house is free of images and photographs of animated objects, as well as other things that attract Satans.

❖ That the patient prays all five obligatory prayers every day, punctually, without qadaa (delay).

The following things must be done daily:

❖ The patient must recite all Adhkaar mentioned under "basic safety measures" at the times mentioned. (One can also add more authentic Adhkaar if one wishes.) That means one recites every morning and every evening, as well as every night before going to sleep, the Adhkaar as described.

❖ The patient must read the Qur'ân at least 45 minutes per day (best twice or thrice a day) with the intention of Ruqya. It must be read at least al-Fatihah, Ayat-ul-Kursi, al-Ikhlas, al-Falaq and an-Naas, repeated if necessary to fill the time. If the patient is not able to read on himself, then someone else has to read on him. If there is no other choice, one can also play Ruqya audio files[18] or use them as a supplement, although this is not ideal.

❖ The patient must often remember Allāh, turn to Him and ask for His help, e.g. with the following du'a:

$$\text{لَّا إِلَهَ إِلَّا أَنتَ سُبْحَانَكَ إِنِّي كُنتُ مِنَ الظَّالِمِينَ}$$

La ilaha illa anta, subhaanaka inni kuntu minath-tholimien

"There is no God but thou: glory to thee: I was indeed among the wrongdoers!" [Al-Anbiya 87]

$$\text{أَنِّي مَسَّنِيَ الضُّرُّ وَأَنتَ أَرْحَمُ الرَّاحِمِينَ}$$

Anni massaniyadh-dhurru wa anta arhamur-rahimien

"Truly distress has seized me, but Thou art the Most Merciful of those that are merciful." [Anbiya 83]

---

[18] http://www.youtube.com/watch?v=ve3I2jiBUTk

The following things have to be done weekly:

❖ The patient must read Sura al-Baqarah in his house, no less than once every three days. It would be preferable if al-Baqarah would be integrated into the daily Ruqya, but that depends on a person's ability. If a person is not able to, then as described above.

The following things must be done monthly:

❖ The patient must implement the 7-day program at least once a month, preferably twice.

The following things should be done regularly:

❖ The patient should be cupped regularly (cupping means in Arabic *Hijamah*). One should inform the practitioner about one's specific problem and follow the practitioner's recommendations. If Hijamah is not possible, one should support the Ruqya with fasting (e.g. on Mondays and Thursdays), or sweating for detoxifying (e.g. by doing sports). Of course one should also pay attention to the diet (*halal* and *thayyib*).

❖ One can support the treatment with the Ruqya bath, which will be explained in the next chapter, if this does not become too strenuous.

The Ruqya bath against Sihr

Ruqya baths are a very effective method to weaken the effects of magic. These baths should be an important part of the treatment. One has to motivate oneself and take the trouble to take these baths, because they are definitely worth the time and effort. One should recall that healing comes from Allāh, so one should ask Him to heal one through the baths, and one should do this as regularly as possible.

On YouTube, there is a video[19] that a sister has kindly uploaded, illustrating how to do the Ruqya bath.

There are a few different variants of the Ruqya bath, but they are all quite similar. The ingredients can vary (see "Variation of the Ruqya Bath" below).

One should not postpone the bath unnecessarily if one does not have a certain ingredient. The most important is anyway the recitation of the Qur'an on the water. Here, too, one should not go into extremes and let Satan induce doubts, e.g. that the pronunciation of the Arabic might not be good enough so that the Ruqya would be ineffective. If one makes efforts, Allāh will make the Rukyah work by His permission.

---

[19] https://www.youtube.com/DqklNcAvCRQ

Ingredients:

- Saffron – 3 pinches
- Sidr (lote tree) leaves. 7 leaves, or 7 pinches if it is in powder form
- 3 table spoons of Apple cider vinegar
- Dead sea salt (coarse, not powdered)
- Orange blossom water
- Rosewater
- 1 litre of Water

Most of these ingredients can be found in 'middle eastern' or 'ethnic foods' store, or can be ordered on the internet.

Method:

On all the ingredients should be recited. One can either recite on the ingredients individually in their own bottles or one can put the ingredients in a bowl and recite on the mixture. This is better because the shorter the time between recitation and usage, the more effective it is. One should recite (in Arabic) and then blow on the mixture, but with little spit, e.g. by slightly moistening the lips:

Al-Fatitah – The Opening (7-times)

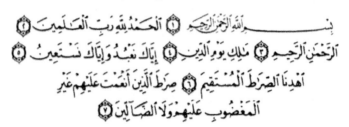

Bismillah-hir-rahman nir rahiem. Al-hamdulillah-hir-rabbil a'lameen, ar-rahman nir-raheem, maliki yaumid-deen. Iyyaka na' budu' wa iyyaka nasta'in. Ihdinas-sirathal mustaqeem, sirathal-lasina an amta alaihim, ghairil maghduubi alaihim wa lad-dhaalleen.

In the name of Allah, the Beneficent, the Merciful. Praise be to Allah, Lord of the Worlds, The Beneficent, the Merciful, Master of the Day of Judgment, Thee [alone] we worship; Thee [alone] we ask for help. Show us the straight path, the path of those whom Thou hast favoured; Not the [path] of those who earn Thine anger nor of those who go astray.

Al-Baqarah – The Cow 1-5

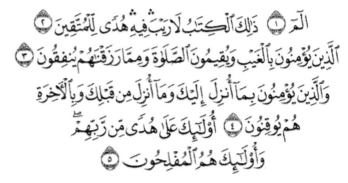

Alif lam miem. Salikal kitabu la ghaiba fiehi hudal-lil muttaqien. Allasina yu'minuuna bil ghaibi wa yuqiemuunash-sholata wa mimma rasaqnaahum yunfiquun. Wallasina yu'minuuna bimaa unsila ilaika wa maa unsila min qablika wa bil achirati hum yuuqinuun. Ulaaika 'ala hudam-mir-rabbihim, wa ulaaika humul muflihuun.

Alif Laam Miem. This is the Book; in it is guidance sure, without doubt, to those who fear Allah; Who believe in the Unseen, are steadfast in prayer, and spend out of what We have provided for them; And who believe in the Revelation sent to thee, and sent before thy time, and [in their earts] have the assurance of the Hereafter. They are on [true] guidance, from their Lord, and it is these who will prosper.

Al-Baqarah 102 (7-times)

وَٱتَّبَعُواْ مَا تَتْلُواْ ٱلشَّيَٰطِينُ عَلَىٰ مُلْكِ سُلَيْمَٰنَ وَمَا كَفَرَ سُلَيْمَٰنُ وَلَٰكِنَّ ٱلشَّيَٰطِينَ كَفَرُواْ يُعَلِّمُونَ ٱلنَّاسَ ٱلسِّحْرَ وَمَا أُنزِلَ عَلَى ٱلْمَلَكَيْنِ بِبَابِلَ هَٰرُوتَ وَمَٰرُوتَ وَمَا يُعَلِّمَانِ مِنْ أَحَدٍ حَتَّىٰ يَقُولَا إِنَّمَا نَحْنُ فِتْنَةٌ فَلَا تَكْفُرْ فَيَتَعَلَّمُونَ مِنْهُمَا مَا يُفَرِّقُونَ بِهِۦ بَيْنَ ٱلْمَرْءِ وَزَوْجِهِۦ وَمَا هُم بِضَآرِّينَ بِهِۦ مِنْ أَحَدٍ إِلَّا بِإِذْنِ ٱللَّهِ وَيَتَعَلَّمُونَ مَا يَضُرُّهُمْ وَلَا يَنفَعُهُمْ وَلَقَدْ عَلِمُواْ لَمَنِ ٱشْتَرَٮٰهُ مَا لَهُۥ فِى ٱلْآخِرَةِ مِنْ خَلَٰقٍ وَلَبِئْسَ مَا شَرَوْاْ بِهِۦ أَنفُسَهُمْ لَوْ كَانُواْ يَعْلَمُونَ ۞

Wattaba'uu maa tatlusch-shayaathienu 'ala mulki sulaimaan, wa maa kafara sulaimaanu wa laakinnash-shayaathiena kafaruu yu'allimuunan-naasas-sihra wa maa unsila 'alal malakaini bibaabila haaruuta wa maaruut, wa maa yu'allimaani min ahadin hatta yaqula innimaa nahnu fitnatun fala takfur, fayat'allamuuna minhumaa maa yufarriquunabihi bainal mari wa saujihi, wa maa hum bidhaar-rienabihi min ahadin illa bi isnillah, wa yata'allamuuna maa ya dhurruhum wa la yanfu'uhum, wa laqad 'alimuulamanish taraahu maa lahu, fil achirati min chalaaq, wa la bi'sa maa sharaubihi anfusahum, lau kaanuu ya'lahuun.

They followed what the evil ones gave out [falsely] against the power of Solomon: the blasphemers were not Solomon, but the evil ones, teaching men Magic, and such things as came down at Babylon to the angels Harut and Marut. But neither of these taught anyone [Such things] without saying: "We are only for trial; so do not blaspheme." They learned from them the means to sow discord between man and wife. But they could not thus harm anyone except by Allah's permission. And they learned what harmed them, not what profited them. And they knew that the buyers of [magic] would have no share in the happiness of the Hereafter. And vile was the price for which they did sell their souls, if they but knew!

Al-Baqarah 255 – Ayat-ul-kursi

اللَّهُ لَا إِلَٰهَ إِلَّا هُوَ الْحَيُّ الْقَيُّومُ لَا تَأْخُذُهُ سِنَةٌ وَلَا نَوْمٌ لَّهُ مَا فِي السَّمَاوَاتِ وَمَا فِي الْأَرْضِ مَن ذَا الَّذِي يَشْفَعُ عِندَهُ إِلَّا بِإِذْنِهِ يَعْلَمُ مَا بَيْنَ أَيْدِيهِمْ وَمَا خَلْفَهُمْ وَلَا يُحِيطُونَ بِشَيْءٍ مِّنْ عِلْمِهِ إِلَّا بِمَا شَاءَ وَسِعَ كُرْسِيُّهُ السَّمَاوَاتِ وَالْأَرْضَ وَلَا يَئُودُهُ حِفْظُهُمَا وَهُوَ الْعَلِيُّ الْعَظِيمُ ﴿٢٥٥﴾

Allāhu – la ilaaha illa huwal hayyul qayyuum, la ta'chusuhu sinatuw-wa la naum, lahu maa fis-samawaati wa maa fil ardh, man salasi yashfa'u 'indahu illa bi isni, ya'lamu maa baina aidihim wa maa chalfahum, wa la yuhiethuuna bi shaim-min 'ilmihi illa bimaa shaa-a, wa si'a kursiyuhus-samawaati wal ardh, wa la ya uduhu hifsahuma, wa huwal 'aliyul 'athiem.

Allah! There is no god but He,-the Living, the Self-subsisting, Eternal. No slumber can seize Him nor sleep. His are all things in the heavens and on earth. Who is there can intercede in His presence except as He permitteth? He knoweth what [appeareth to His creatures as] before or after or behind them. Nor shall they compass aught of His knowledge except as He willeth. His Throne doth extend over the heavens and the earth, and He feeleth no fatigue in guarding and preserving them for He is the Most High, the Supreme [in glory].

Al-Baqarah 256

لَآ إِكْرَاهَ فِى ٱلدِّينِ قَد تَّبَيَّنَ ٱلرُّشْدُ مِنَ ٱلْغَيِّ فَمَن يَكْفُرْ بِٱلطَّٰغُوتِ وَيُؤْمِنۢ بِٱللَّهِ فَقَدِ ٱسْتَمْسَكَ بِٱلْعُرْوَةِ ٱلْوُثْقَىٰ لَا ٱنفِصَامَ لَهَاۗ وَٱللَّهُ سَمِيعٌ عَلِيمٌ ۝

Laa ikraha fid-dien, qad-tabaiyanar-rushdu minal ghaiy, faman yakfur bithooghuuti wa yu'mim billahi faqadis-tamsaka bil'urwatil-wusqaa lanfishoomalaha, wAllāhu sami'un 'aliem.

Let there be no compulsion in religion: Truth stands out clear from Error: whoever rejects evil and believes in Allah hath grasped the most trustworthy hand-hold that never breaks. And Allah heareth and knoweth all things.

Al-Baqarah 257

ٱللَّهُ وَلِىُّ ٱلَّذِينَ ءَامَنُواْ يُخْرِجُهُم مِّنَ ٱلظُّلُمَٰتِ إِلَى ٱلنُّورِ وَٱلَّذِينَ كَفَرُوٓاْ أَوْلِيَآؤُهُمُ ٱلطَّٰغُوتُ يُخْرِجُونَهُم مِّنَ ٱلنُّورِ إِلَى ٱلظُّلُمَٰتِ أُوْلَٰٓئِكَ أَصْحَٰبُ ٱلنَّارِ هُمْ فِيهَا خَٰلِدُونَ ۝

Allāhu waliyyul-lasina amanu yuchrijuhum-minath-thulumaati ilan-nur, wallasina kafaruu auliyaa wuhumuth-thaaghuutu yuchriju nahum-minan-nuri ilath-thulumaat, uulaaika ash-haabun-nar, hum fieha chaliduun.

Allah is the Protector of those who have faith: from the depths of darkness He will lead them forth into light. Of those who reject faith the patrons are the evil ones: from light they will lead them forth into the depths of darkness. They will be companions of the fire, to dwell therein [For ever].

Al-Baqarah 284

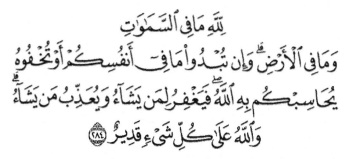

Lillahi maa fis-samawaati wa maa fil ardh, wa intubduumaa fie anfusikum autuchfuuhu yuhaasibkum bihilla, fayaghfiru limaiyashaa-u wa yu'asibu maiyashaa, wAllāhu ala kulli shain qadier.

To Allah belongeth all that is in the heavens and on earth. Whether ye show what is in your minds or conceal it, Allah Calleth you to account for it. He forgiveth whom He pleaseth, and punisheth whom He pleaseth, for Allah hath power over all things.

Al-Baqarah 285

ءَامَنَ ٱلرَّسُولُ بِمَآ أُنزِلَ إِلَيْهِ مِن رَّبِّهِۦ وَٱلْمُؤْمِنُونَ ۚ كُلٌّ ءَامَنَ بِٱللَّهِ وَمَلَٰٓئِكَتِهِۦ وَكُتُبِهِۦ وَرُسُلِهِۦ لَا نُفَرِّقُ بَيْنَ أَحَدٍ مِّن رُّسُلِهِۦ ۚ وَقَالُوا۟ سَمِعْنَا وَأَطَعْنَا ۖ غُفْرَانَكَ رَبَّنَا وَإِلَيْكَ ٱلْمَصِيرُ ۝

Amanar-rasuulu bimaa unsila ilaihi mir-rabbihi wal mu'minuun, kullun amana billahi wa malaaikatihi wa kutubihi wa rasulihi, la nufar-riqu baina ahadim-mirrusulihi, wa qaalu sami'na wa atho'naa ghufraanaka wa ilaikal mashier.

The Messenger believeth in what hath been revealed to him from his Lord, as do the men of faith. Each one [of them] believeth in Allah, His angels, His books, and His messengers. "We make no distinction [they say] between one and another of His messengers." And they say: "We hear, and we obey: [We seek] Thy forgiveness, our Lord, and to Thee is the end of all journeys."

Al-Baqarah 286

لَا يُكَلِّفُ
ٱللَّهُ نَفْسًا إِلَّا وُسْعَهَا لَهَا مَا كَسَبَتْ وَعَلَيْهَا مَا ٱكْتَسَبَتْ
رَبَّنَا لَا تُؤَاخِذْنَآ إِن نَّسِينَآ أَوْ أَخْطَأْنَا رَبَّنَا وَلَا تَحْمِلْ
عَلَيْنَآ إِصْرًا كَمَا حَمَلْتَهُۥ عَلَى ٱلَّذِينَ مِن قَبْلِنَا رَبَّنَا
وَلَا تُحَمِّلْنَا مَا لَا طَاقَةَ لَنَا بِهِۦ وَٱعْفُ عَنَّا وَٱغْفِرْ لَنَا
وَٱرْحَمْنَآ أَنتَ مَوْلَىٰنَا فَٱنصُرْنَا عَلَى ٱلْقَوْمِ ٱلْكَٰفِرِينَ ﴿٢٨٦﴾

La yukallifullahu nafsan illa wus'aha, laha maa kasabat wa 'alaihaa maktasabat, rabbana la tuaachisnaa in-nasiena au achtho'na, rabbana wa la tahmil 'alaina ishran kamaa hamaltahu 'alallasina min qoblina, rabbana wa la tuhammilna maa la thaa qatalanabihi, wa'fu'anna, waghfirlana, warhamna, anta maulaana fanshurnaa 'alal qaumil kaafirien.

On no soul doth Allah Place a burden greater than it can bear. It gets every good that it earns, and it suffers every ill that it earns. [Pray:] "Our Lord! Condemn us not if we forget or fall into error; our Lord! Lay not on us a burden Like that which Thou didst lay on those before us; Our Lord! Lay not on us a burden greater than we have strength to bear. Blot out our sins, and grant us forgiveness. Have mercy on us. Thou art our Protector; Help us against those who stand against faith."

Al-Araf – The heights 117-122

وَأَوْحَيْنَا إِلَىٰ مُوسَىٰ أَنْ أَلْقِ عَصَاكَ فَإِذَا هِيَ تَلْقَفُ مَا يَأْفِكُونَ ۞
۩ فَوَقَعَ ٱلْحَقُّ وَبَطَلَ مَا كَانُوا يَعْمَلُونَ ۞ فَغُلِبُوا
هُنَالِكَ وَٱنقَلَبُوا صَٰغِرِينَ ۞ وَأُلْقِيَ ٱلسَّحَرَةُ سَٰجِدِينَ ۞
قَالُوا ءَامَنَّا بِرَبِّ ٱلْعَٰلَمِينَ ۞ رَبِّ مُوسَىٰ وَهَٰرُونَ ۞

Wa au hainaa ila muusa an alqi 'ashoka fa isa hiya talqafu maa ya'fikum. Fawaqa'alhaqqu wa bathola maa kaanuu ya'maluun. Faghulibuu hunaalika wanqalabuu shoghirien. Walqiyas-saharatu saajidien. Qaaluu amanna birabbil'aalamien. Rabbi muusa wa haaruun.

We put it into Moses's mind by inspiration: "Throw [now] thy rod": and behold! it swallows up straight away all the falsehoods which they fake!. Thus truth was confirmed, and all that they did was made of no effect. So the [great ones] were vanquished there and then, and were made to look small. But the sorcerers fell down prostrate in adoration. Saying: "We believe in the Lord of the Worlds, - "The Lord of Moses and Aaron."

Yunus – Jonas 79-82

وَقَالَ فِرْعَوْنُ ٱئْتُونِي بِكُلِّ سَٰحِرٍ عَلِيمٍ ۞ فَلَمَّا جَآءَ ٱلسَّحَرَةُ
قَالَ لَهُم مُّوسَىٰ أَلْقُوا مَآ أَنتُم مُّلْقُونَ ۞ فَلَمَّا أَلْقَوْا قَالَ
مُوسَىٰ مَا جِئْتُم بِهِ ٱلسِّحْرُ إِنَّ ٱللَّهَ سَيُبْطِلُهُ إِنَّ ٱللَّهَ لَا يُصْلِحُ
عَمَلَ ٱلْمُفْسِدِينَ ۞ وَيُحِقُّ ٱللَّهُ ٱلْحَقَّ بِكَلِمَٰتِهِ وَلَوْ كَرِهَ
ٱلْمُجْرِمُونَ ۞

Wa qaala fira'unu'tuni bikulli saahirin 'aliem. Falamma dschaa as-saharatu qaala lahum muusa alquu maa antum mulquun. Falamma alqau qaala muusa maa dschi'tum bihis-sihru, innAllāha sayubthiluhu, innAllāha la yushlihu 'amalal mufsiduun. Wa yuhiqqullahul haqqa bikalimaatihi, wa lau karihal mudschrimuun.

Said Pharaoh: "Bring me every sorcerer well versed." When the sorcerers came, Moses said to them: "Throw ye what ye [wish] to throw!" When they had had their throw, Moses said: "What ye have brought is sorcery: Allah will surely make it of no effect: for Allah prospereth not the work of those who make mischief." And Allah by His words doth prove and establish His truth, however much the sinners may hate it!

Taha 65-69

قَالُوا يَٰمُوسَىٰٓ إِمَّآ أَن تُلْقِىَ وَإِمَّآ أَن نَّكُونَ أَوَّلَ مَنْ أَلْقَىٰ ۝ قَالَ بَلْ أَلْقُوا فَإِذَا حِبَالُهُمْ وَعِصِيُّهُمْ يُخَيَّلُ إِلَيْهِ مِن سِحْرِهِمْ أَنَّهَا تَسْعَىٰ ۝ فَأَوْجَسَ فِى نَفْسِهِۦ خِيفَةً مُّوسَىٰ ۝ قُلْنَا لَا تَخَفْ إِنَّكَ أَنتَ ٱلْأَعْلَىٰ ۝ وَأَلْقِ مَا فِى يَمِينِكَ تَلْقَفْ مَا صَنَعُوٓا إِنَّمَا صَنَعُوا كَيْدُ سَٰحِرٍ وَلَا يُفْلِحُ ٱلسَّاحِرُ حَيْثُ أَتَىٰ ۝

Qaaluu yaa muusa imma an tulqiya wa imma an-nakuuna auwala man alqa. Qaala bal alquu, fa isa hibaaluhum wa 'ishiyuhum yuchaiyalu ilaihi min sihrihim annahaa tas'aa. Fa audschasa fie nafsihi chiefatam-muusa. Qulnaa la tachaf innaka antal 'ala. Wa alqi maa fie yamienika talqaf maa shana'uu, innamaa shana'uu kaidu saahirin wa la yuflihus-saahiru haisu ataa.

They said: "O Moses! whether wilt thou that thou throw [first] or that we be the first to throw?" He said, "Nay, throw ye first!" Then behold their ropes and their rods-so it seemed to him on account of their magic - began to be in lively motion! So Moses conceived in his mind a [sort of] fear. We said: "Fear not! for thou hast indeed the upper hand: "Throw that which is in thy right hand: Quickly will it swallow up that which they have faked what they have faked is but a magician's trick: and the magician thrives not, [no matter] where he goes."

Al-Ikhlas – Purity of Faith

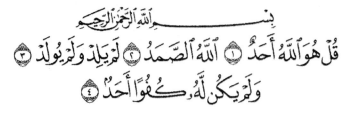

Qul huwal-lahu ahad, al-lahus-samad, lam yalid wa lamyuulad, wa lam yakul-lahu kufu-wan ahad.

Say: He is Allah, the One and Only; Allah, the Eternal, Absolute; He begetteth not, nor is He begotten; and there is none like unto Him.

Al-Falaq – The dawn

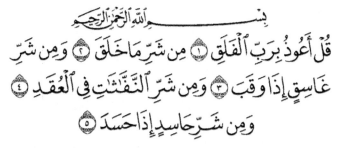

Qul a'usu birabbil falaq, min scharri maa chalaq, wa min scharri ghaasiqin isa waqab, wa min scharrin-naffaasaati fil 'uqad. Wa min sharri hasideen isa hasad.

Say: I seek refuge with the Lord of the Dawn From the mischief of created things; from the mischief of Darkness as it overspreads; from the mischief of those who practise secret arts; and from the mischief of the envious one as he practises envy.

An-Naas – Mankind

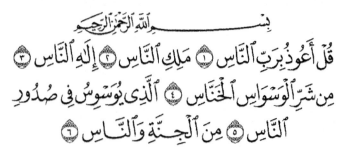

Qul 'ausubirabbin-naas, malikin-naas, ilaahin-naas, min sharril waswaasil channaas, allasi yuwaswisu fie shuduurin-naas, minal Jinnati wan-naas.

Say: I seek refuge with the Lord and Cherisher of Mankind, The King of Mankind, The god [or judge] of Mankind, from the mischief of the Whisperer [of Evil], who withdraws [after his whisper], [The same] who whispers into the hearts of Mankind, Among Jinn and among men.

Take a small amount of Apple cider vinegar and massage it into your head, enough to cover your scalp/hair.

Fill up your bath with warm water from the tap as you would if you were having a normal bath. Pour the contents of the bowl/ingredients into the bath. Sit in the bath for 30 minutes and submerge yourself as much as you can in the water.

After some time (10/20 minutes) take the bowl and pour the water over your head at least three times or as much as possible. This will wash out the cider vinegar from your hair. You should take the bath in the evening, because Jinn are more active at night, so they are then combated when they are just waking up, and one is better protected when they are active.

This is the best and most effective method. If you follow these instructions, you will feel a difference, inshaAllāh.

It is important to continue with the daily safety measures, to do the obligatory prayers on time, and to read as much as possible Qur'an, especially Sura al-Baqarah. The etiquettes for sleeping should be observed to one's best ability (see appendix) and the daily Dhikr.

IMPORTANT:

You may hesitate to get into the bath – this is shaytaan doing his utmost to put doubts in your mind and put you off doing the bath as, by Allah's will, it will weaken and hurt them. If you feel yourself hesitating or doubting, say '*Bismillah*' and go forth. Don't think about it, just go ahead and do it.

It is possible that you may feel like you are in pain and that the bath is causing you pain. This is actually a GOOD sign because this means your body is healing inshaAllāh. One should then do his best and try to endure the pain. Even if you do not feel pain or something else, you should continue with the bath.

Do the baths for seven days in a row. Don't falter – be strong in your resolve and have confidence that Allah will help you through the recitation and the Ruqya which you have done. After seven days you should continue with the bath as often as possible but at least once every two days. The more you do it the better.

Sometimes it is necessary to support the treatment with hijamah (cupping) so that the magic can get out. You have to put the cupping head as close as possible to where the symptoms are.

Hijamah is not difficult and harmless when practiced with some care. However, it would go beyond the purpose of this book to explain the techniques more closely. Yet, it should not be difficult to learn basic knowledge over the Internet and to consult a practitioner.

Variant of the Ruqya bath and cleaning of the house of Jinn or Sihr

Take 20 liters of water (preferably rainwater, as there are most probably no 20 liters of Zam-Zam water available) and recite the same verses as mentioned in the previous chapter and blow / spit on the water like described. This each 11 times.

Drink two glasses of this water.

Two glasses pour into the bath water and bath or shower with it.

Two glasses of the water are poured into a small bucket of water, stir and then fill the water into a spray bottle like one uses for flowers. Then spray the interior of the whole house, also under the furniture, in the oven, washing machine, sink, fireplace, windows and doors (also the outside), especially the door threshold of the entrance door and the marriage bed. In the bathroom, first close the toilet and then sprinkle the rest. Outside only the windows, doors and corners of the house. If you have a business, especially the warehouse where the goods are kept, and all machines.

It is important to say "*Bismillah*" before spraying, so that the Jinn have the opportunity to avoid the water and are not burnt by it, because it could hit believing Jinn and those who not do evil.

This is done for 11 days. If the 20 liters are finished, prepare another 20 liters.

One should not be amazed or frightened when one hears sighs, sees smoke as if something would burn, one smells burned things or sees dying animals in one's dream (rats, snakes, lizards, etc). This is a sign that the Ruqya has worked.

In addition, candles can be recited on, preferably scented candles. Recite on them 30 times Ayat-ul-kursi, ignite them and let them burn for an hour in every room. This can also be done with wood, which is burned in the fireplace.

Waswasah – whisperings

A number of patients complain about severe whisperings, known in Arabic as *waswasah*. These can take the form of voices or compulsive thoughts. These thoughts are often blasphemous and can be extremely disturbing for the patient, so disturbing even that many people question their faith.

While Ruqya is an important means of treatment, there are still some other things that can be done. With the grace of Allāh and His mercy, the thoughts will disappear within about a week with these simple steps:

1. Realize that the thoughts come from Shaitan. One should not think that one is an evil person or is responsible for these things. The proof of this is the statement of the Prophet ﷺ: "Allah, may He be glorified and exalted, will forgive my ummah for whatever crosses their minds, as long as they do not act upon it or speak of it."[20]

2. Realize that such thoughts have plagued even some of the Prophet's companions.

   Abu Hurayrah رضي الله عن ه *reported that some of the people of the messenger of Allāh* ﷺ *came to him and said: ,Indeed we perceive in our minds that which every one of us considers too grave to express'. He replied, "Do you really perceive it?" They said, "Yes." He said, "That is true faith."*[21]

   Ibn 'Abbās رضي الله عن ه *narated that a man came to the Messenger* ﷺ *and said, "O Messenger of Allah!*

---

[20] Bukhāri and Muslim
[21] Muslim

One of us has thoughts of such a nature that he would rather be reduced to charcoal than speak about them." The Messenger (may the peace and blessings of Allāh be upon him) said, "Allāh is the Greatest! Allāh is the Greatest! Allāh is the Greatest! All praise be to Allah who has reduced [the shaytān's] plot to whispering."[22]

3. Take the steps already mentioned to protect yourself from the Satans. The house is also to be protected by reciting al-Baqarah and removing everything that the Jinn attracts, such as TV, music, pictures and photos. One should also carry out the 7-day program.

4. One must persistently reject these thoughts, and it is important that one does this every time.

When such thoughts appear, do the following:

❖ Mention the greatness of Allāh and his perfection, either by saying *Allāhu Akbar* or *SubhānAllāh*.

❖ Seek refuge with Allāh from Satan by saying *A'udhu billāhi min ash-shaytānir-rajim* or something similar:

$$ \text{أَعُوذُ بِاللهِ مِنَ الشَّيْطَانِ الرَّجِيمِ} $$

I seek refuge with Allāh from Satan, the outcast. [23]

❖ Confirm your faith in Allāh and His Messenger ﷺ by reciting the following Adhkaar:

$$ \text{آمَنْتُ بِاللهِ وَرُسُلِهِ} $$

Aamantu billaahi wa rusulihi

---

[22] Abu Dawood
[23] Muslim 2203

I have believed in Allāh and His Messenger. [24]

$$\text{هُوَ الأَوَّلُ ، وَالآخِرُ ، وَالظَّاهِرُ}$$
$$\text{وَالْبَاطِنُ ، وَهُوَ بِكُلِّ شَيْءٍ عَلِيمٌ}$$

Huwal-auwalu, wal-aakhiru, waẓ-ẓaahiru, wal-baaṭinu, wa huwa bi kulli shay'in 'alim

He is the first and the last and the outer and the inner, and He knows all things. [25]

❖ Seek Allāh's forgiveness, either with a simple *Astaghfirullāh* or something more:

$$\text{أَسْتَغْفِرُ اللهَ الَّذِي لَا إِلَهَ إِلَّا هُوَ الْحَيُّ الْقَيُّومُ وَأَتُوبُ إِلَيْهِ}$$

Astaghfirullaa-hal-ladhi laa ilaha illaa huwal-ḥayyul-qayyum wa atubu ilayh

I seek forgiveness in Allāh, no one has the right to be worshiped except Him, the living One, the Eternal, and I turn to Him in repentance. [26]

$$\text{«اللَّهُمَّ أَنتَ رَبِّي، لَا إِلَهَ إِلاَّ أَنتَ، خَلَقْتَنِي وأَنا عَبْدُكَ، وأَنا عَلَى عهْدِكَ}$$
$$\text{ووَعْدِكَ مَا اسْتَطَعْتُ، أَعوذُ بِكَ مِنْ شَرِّ مَا صنَعْتُ، أَبوءُ لكَ بِنِعْمَتِكَ}$$
$$\text{عَلَيَّ، وَأَبوءُ بِذَنْبِي، فَاغْفِرْ لِي، فَإِنَّهُ لا يغْفِرُ الذُّنوبَ إِلاَّ أَنتَ.»}$$

Allāhumma anta Rabbi, la ilaha illa anta, khalaqtani, wa ana 'abduka, wa ana' ala 'ahdika wa wa'dika mastata't, authubika min sharri ma sana't, abu'u laka bi ni'matika alayya, wa abu 'u bisanbi, faghfirli, fa innahu la yaghfiruth thunuba illa ant.

O Allāh, Thou art my Lord, there is no God but thyself. Thou hast created me, and I am thy servant, and I try to fulfill my agreement

---

[24] Muslim 134
[25] Abu Dawood 5110
[26] Abu Dawood 1517; At-Tirmidhi 3577

and my promise to thee as best I can. I seek my refuge with you from the evil of my actions. I bear witness to the good which you have done to me, and I bear witness to my sins, therefore forgive me, for no one can forgive sins except you. [27]

This dhikr is the best for asking forgiveness from Allāh. The Prophet ﷺ said, whoever says this dhikr in the morning and dies that day goes to paradise, and whoever says it in the evening and dies in that night goes to paradise.

Even if the thoughts themselves are not a sin, it is a good habit to get in to asking forgiveness, and there are several reports of the companions seeking forgiveness for things in which it isn't clear that they did anything wrong. Furthermore, seeking Allāh's forgiveness frequently will push the shaytān away from you and make you closer to Allāh, as well as putting your mind at ease when you feel a degree of responsibility for these thoughts.

There shouldn't be any Jinn, no matter how persistent, who can bear this over a prolonged period, and when used in addition to Ruqya, the seven day program, and while protecting yourself and your house, your problems will disappear, by the permission of Allāh, the Exalted.

---

[27] Bukhari, Muslim and others

Overcoming addiction to pornography and "similar addictions"

One of the most common questions asked relates to overcoming the addiction to pornography and what one might call politely "related addictions". It is not a beautiful subject, and if it does not apply to you, then praise Allāh that He has not tried you with something He has examined so many of His servants.

Pray! The following Du'a was made by the Prophet ﷺ for a boy who longed to commit Zinā.

Only the first person was replaced with the third:

اللهُمَّ اغْفِرْ ذَنْبِي وَطَهِّرْ قَلْبِي، وَحَصِّنْ فَرْجِي

Allāhum-magh-fir dhan-bi wa ṭah-hir qal-bi, wa ḥaṣṣin far-ji

O Allāh, forgive my sin, clean my heart and protect my chastity. [28]

Or the following:

اللَّهُمَّ إِنِّي أَعُوذُ بِكَ مِنْ شَرِّ سَمْعِي، وَمِنْ شَرِّ بَصَرِي، وَمِنْ شَرِّ لِسَانِي، وَمِنْ شَرِّ قَلْبِي، وَمِنْ شَرِّ مَنِيِّي

Allāhumma in-ni a'udhu bi-ka min shar-ri sam'i, wa min shar-ri baṣa-ri, wa min shar-ri li-saani, wa min shar-ri qal-bi, wa min sharri mani-yi

---

[28] Ahmad 22211

O Allāh, I seek refuge with you from hearing evil, and from seeing evil, and from speaking evil, from the evil of my heart, and the evil of my carnal desires. [29]

One should recognize the severity of sin in general and the severity of this particular sin and develop a hatred for it one's heart. Allāh has told us that the rightly guided people hate defiance and disobedience.

> ... but Allah hath endeared the faith to you and hath beautified it in your hearts, and hath made disbelief and lewdness and rebellion hateful unto you. Such are they who are the rightly guided. [Hujurat 7]

One should develop a revulsion from this kind of disobedience, whatever temporary pleasure that it gives. This, in itself, is a struggle, so don't expect it to be easy.

One should check one's prayer. Whenever one falls into sins, which can be termed as "faḥshaa" - immorality - you have to ask yourself whether there is something missing in the prayer: missed prayers, delayed prayers, not responding to the adhaan, and prayers without concentration are all a problem. Prayer prevents immorality and wrongdoing, so if it isn't doing the job, then it's most likely not being done in the right way.

> Lo! worship preserveth from lewdness and iniquity, but verily remembrance of Allah is more important. And Allah knoweth what ye do. [Al-Ankabut 45]

One should repent at once, and this repentance should be sincere: one never does it again, and one implores Allāh to help one. Yes, it is possible that one slips and falls again, but the stronger the determination to leave this sin, the better it will be.

---

[29] Abu Dawood 1551 At-Tirmidhi 3492 An-Nasa'i 5444, 5455

One should separate oneself from the things that make one commit this sin, even if it means that one exchanges the smartphone for a simple mobile phone, disconnects from the broadband, moves the computer into the living room or does something else. When one is serious about repentance, one is ready to take serious steps. One should also consider whether "adult-content" can be blocked by settings on the computer, e.g. with a random, long password that one can not remember and does not record. Certainly, these are only small measures, and a determined person can by-pass them, but the more one does, the harder it will be, and the more determined you become yourself.

One should be around good people. These sins are sins that are almost exclusively committed alone. The less you are alone, the better the chance of breaking the habit. Consider sharing your room, if that's an option; share your phone and computer with others, so that there is less privacy.

But if one is alone and is afraid to fall back into sin, one should not let this thought run its course, but one must get up and leave the private place to break the habit. It is not a substitute for the fear of Allāh, but it is a temporary measure that can take you away from the sin you had intended.

One should regularly fast - at least twice a week, and if one can and if necessary, even every other day. The Prophet ﷺ explained that this restrains the desires, so it is worthwhile to integrate the fast into the overall solution.

If one feels that this problem might be associated with Jinn, one should start with the 7-day program and then go to the full Ruqya program if required. It is rare that these problems are caused solely by Jinn, except in extreme cases. For most people, the Jinn simply uses the already existing desires, which is why one should primarily master these desires.

Of course, marriage also protects against such desires, but it is not an option for most people at the time of their problems, or they are already married and still have these problems.

Jinn attacks at night

Night attacks and sexual assaults by Jinn are reported by a number of patients, and undoubtedly this is one of the most distressing things a patient can suffer. Most patients who report it are women.

These attacks almost always take place during the night while one is in bed, and most often when no one else is in the room. These attacks differ from dreams in the sense that the victim is often awake, as well as the fact that pain and physical effects such as rape are often present the next morning; however, some people experience the same feelings and images as part of a dream, either with or without physical trauma, and the following advice is appropriate for both cases.

Regarding the Islamic faith and what the scholars have said about Jinn, there is no reason to deny that these attacks can take place, both through the medium of dreams and during being awake. This is consistent with what we know about the Jinn, and the reports are numerous and intrinsically trustworthy.

With regard to preventive measures, there are a number of things that can be done both general and specific. The general measures have already been dealt with in the previous chapters, namely the general protective measures and the 7-day Ruqya program. The following are recommended as specific measures:

If one is already strictly adhering to the protective measures, has removed everything from the house which attracts Satans, and recites the recommended Adhkaar, especially those which are said in the morning and in the evening, and those which are said before going to sleep, one can also do the following:

❖ The supplication, which refers to the overcoming of an enemy to be said when you are in fear of an attack taking place (such as before sleeping, or when waking up suddenly at night) or during an attack:

اللّٰهُمَّ إِنَّا نَجْعَلُكَ فِي نُحُورِهِمْ ، وَنَعُوذُ بِكَ مِنْ شُرُورِهِمْ

Allāhumma innaa naj'aluka fie nuḥurihim, wa na'udhu bika min shururihim.

O Allāh, we set you before them, and we seek refuge with you from their evil.[30]

❖ Taking a Ruqya bath before sleeping, as described on page 62 onwards.

❖ Rubbing oneself with Ruqya oil before sleeping. The production of the Ruqya oil is described on page 57 onwards.

❖ Waking up for the night prayer (Tahajjud), for when Satan knows that one is responding to night attacks by doing one of the greatest voluntary forms of worship, then the incentive to attack one becomes considerably less; not to mention the general virtue of praying the night prayer, in terms of acceptance of supplications, and so on.

❖ Observing the etiquettes of bad dreams and nightmares, for those who experience attacks as part of a dream. See the chapter "Sleeping Etiquettes" in

---

[30] Abu Dawud 1537; Al-Hakim 2629

appendix. Try to recite the verse of the throne 11 times before going to sleep.

❖ It is possible that having someone else in the room at night may help. There is no confirmed evidence, and it does not seem to affect the dreams, but it seems that people who suffer physical attacks while they are awake are mostly people who sleep alone, so it's worth mentioning here, without giving too much importance to it.

Psoriasis, eczema and other ailments

Many people ask if psoriasis and eczema can be symptomatic of magic or the evil eye, and of course the answer is "maybe." Like a whole host of other symptoms, including headache, nausea, vomiting and insomnia, there is an overlap between genuine medical conditions that have no spiritual cause, and those caused by Jinn and related things.

In essence, we are looking for signs that the disease is outside the usual medical pattern, especially if medical examinations have already taken place but no exact causes could be identified.

There is, of course, a simple solution to such problems, which is also proposed by Ibnul-Qayyim and others, to treat the disease on both a medical and spiritual basis. After all, both of us were given to us by Allāh سبحانه و تعالى as a means of finding a cure, and there is much less contradiction (or contraindication) between the two than could be imagined. For example, could a doctor rightly claim that 45 minutes of reciting the Qur'an every day is considered a contraindication to any sort of modern medicine? Sure, there are extreme cases, e.g. in the case of "mental diseases", during which the patient gets into a rage and Western medicine wants to immobilize him with heavy psychopharmaceuticals, which makes treatment by a Raqi virtually impossible. But these are rare cases.

Nonetheless, whenever possible, any "modern" medicine should be renounced and alternative natural medicine should be used, especially with ingredients recommended by the Prophet ﷺ. Here one can often combine the treatment quite simply.

The following treatment has achieved good results in cases of psoriasis and eczema. Combine these dry ingredients in ground powder form:

➢ 25g henna leaves, known as *Barg-e-Hina*.

➢ 10g blackcrop, known as *Kalonji*.

➢ 10g Senna leaves, known as *Sana Makki*.

➢ 10g *Marine Costus*[31], known in Arabic as *al-Qust al-Bahri* or also as *Qust-e-Shirin*.

Boil all of the dry ingredients together for 15 minutes either in 500 ml of raw organic apple cider vinegar, or in 250 ml olive oil, according to the note below. The liquid will have a strong smell if using the apple cider vinegar, but that is normal. Store the liquid in a glass bottle. You may either sieve it, or let the solids settle at the bottom of the bottle. Put on eczema spots twice a day.

Use apple cider vinegar if the eczema is red like pimples, wet, watery, or bleeding; or olive oil if the eczema has dry white skin peeling off. Apple cider vinegar seems to be more effective in both eczema and psoriasis, including scalp psoriasis. In both cases, it is likely that the ointment will sting the cut & broken skin. With regular use that will subside, inshā'Allāh. The eczema patches should start to dry up and sting less within one week. Use the ointment for 6 months at a stretch, once or twice daily, depending on the severity of the disease. Can be used on all body parts including the scalp & face, but not the eyes.

Separately, try a warm jug of water and add two tablespoons olive oil and pour on the body after each bath, then apply the ointment; this helps to reduce the stinging.

───────────────

[31] https://maher-shop.com/en/beehive/497-marine-costus.html

Magic and the stomach

There is another useful treatment for magic that presents itself through bloating in the stomach, abdominal pain, and/or nausea, and a desire to vomit. Notice that this post is not named 'magic in the stomach', but 'magic and the stomach'. That's because one of the most misdiagnosed things in Ruqya is that the magic has been eaten. While it is true that magic can be fed to a person, this is less common than people imagine it to be. It has reached the extent that some Ruqya practitioners have no other treatment than to say the magic has been fed, and that the person needs to be forced to vomit, through an emetic.

At the same time, there is a legitimate reason why these cases are misdiagnosed, and that is because many forms of magic present themselves through bloating in the stomach, abdominal pain, or nausea. Many patients find a degree of relief from the emetic, and so this fuels the misdiagnosis that a huge portion of people in the world have been fed magic.

An alternative treatment to a strong emetic, but which will - inshā'Allāh - bring the same kind of relief to someone who is suffering from magic that is presenting itself through stomach pains, bloating, or nausea and a desire to vomit. The ingredients are very mild, and are rooted in prophetic medicine, so we hope that it will be better tolerated than the usual means of forcing a patient to vomit. Once again, it should be emphasised that you should consult a medical professional before using these treatments.

- ➢ 1/2 kg of Honey
- ➢ 1 tablespoon of ground Black Seed (*nigella sativa*)
- ➢ 1 tablespoon of ground Meccan Senna
- ➢ 1 tablespoon of ground Rhubarb (also called Rhubarb root powder)
- ➢ 1 tablespoon of ground Cumin

Mix all together, then every morning:

Stir the mixture with a spoon, then bring a cup of water (Zamzam water would be best), and add a tablespoon of the above mixture to it, mix until the honey is dissolved in the water, then drink from it. Do this every day until the mixture finishes.

It is preferred to use Ruqya water, rather than water that has not been recited upon.

Also, one can try mixtures which flush and clean the system. Search google for "Heavy Metal Detox" and "Parasite Detox" - there are a few simple recipes with juices, organic foods etc. They have shown to be a big help for people with Jinn related issues that present as abdominal bloating/pain, and are generally very well tolerated.

Unfulfilled baby desire

Getting no children is a hard test, especially for a woman. It can affect the self-confidence and also the marriage. And for a perilous person, perhaps because of envy, jealousy, or revenge, it may well be a target of black magic. However, experience shows that this is not very often the case. Therefore, it should first be ascertained that this is not a biological problem, i. E. one should consult a specialist. If no biological problem can be identified as a cause for infertility, Ruqya should be considered.

Yet, as always, the most important thing should not be forgotten: getting children is in the hands of Allāh!

> Allāhs is the kingdom of the heavens and the earth. He creates what He wants. He gives girls to whom He pleases, and He gives boys to whom He willth. Or He gives both, boys and girls, and He makes barren whom He willth; He is All-Knowing, Almighty. [As-Sura 49-50]

Whether you can not get children because of a biological or a spiritual problem, it is easy for Allāh to eradicate this problem if He wants. Ḥasan al-Baṣrī had the following advice for couples who remained childless: one should take oneself to account and wonder whether a sin might be the reason why God does not bless one with children, and ask for forgiveness.

> Ask forgiveness from your Lord; Verily, He is Oft-Forgiving; He will send [rain from] the sky upon you in [continuing] showers, and give you increase in wealth and children and provide for you gardens and provide for you rivers. [Nuh 10-12]

The best Du'a for forgiveness is Sayyidul Istighfar:

«اللّٰهُمَّ أنتَ رَبِّي، لا إلٰهَ إلاّ أنتَ، خَلَقْتَنِي وأنا عبدُكَ، وأنا عَلى عهدِكَ
ووَعْدِكَ ما اسْتَطَعْتُ، أَعوذُ بكَ مِنْ شَرِّ ما صَنَعْتُ، أَبوءُ لكَ بِنعْمَتِكَ
عَلَيَّ، وأبوءُ بِذَنْبِي، فاغْفِرْ لِي، فإِنَّهُ لا يغْفِرُ الذُّنوبَ إلاّ أنتَ.»

Allāhumma anta Rabbi, la ilaha illa anta, khalaqtani, wa ana
'abduka, wa ana' ala 'ahdika wa wa'dika mastata't, authubika min
sharri ma sana't, abu'u laka bi ni'matika alayya, wa abu 'u bisanbi,
faghfirli, fa innahu la yaghfiruth thunuba illa ant.

O Allāh, Thou art my Lord, there is no God but thyself. Thou hast
created me, and I am thy servant, and I try to fulfill my agreement
and my promise towards thee as best I can. I seek refuge with you
from the evil of my actions. I bear witness to the good which you
have done to me, and I bear witness to my sins, therefore forgive
me, for no one can forgive sins except you.

One should supplicate especially for the blessing of
having children as the Prophet Zacharias عليه السلام had
done, who was then blessed with the prophet Yahya (John)
عليه السلام:

رَبِّ لَا تَذَرْنِي فَرْدًا وَأَنتَ خَيْرُ الْوَارِثِينَ

Rabbi laa tadharnie fardan wa anta khayr-ul-waarithien.

"My Lord! Leave me not childless, though Thou art the Best of
inheritors." [Al-Anbiya 89]

One should pay attention to prayer and daily
remembrance of Allāh. It is amazing how people master
the worst calamaties with these two things. Allāh says:

*O you who believe! Seek help in patience and
prayer, indeed Allāh is with the patient. [Al-Baqarah
153]*

One should also pay attention to the etiquettes of prayer (see appendix) so that prayer is better accepted by Allāh.

One should thank Allāh for all that He has one given and be content with the determination of Allāh.

And when your Lord proclaimed: If ye give thanks, I will give you more; but if ye are thankless, lo! My punishment is dire. [Ibrahim 7]

Therefore, one should always be grateful and commemorate God in humility so that one is not like those described in the following verses:

He it is Who did create you from a single soul, and therefrom did make his mate that he might take rest in her. And when he covered her she bore a light burden, and she passed [unnoticed] with it, but when it became heavy they cried unto Allah, their Lord, saying: If thou givest unto us aright we shall be of the thankful. But when He gave unto them aright, they ascribed unto Him partners in respect of that which He had given them. High is He Exalted above all that they associate [with Him]. [Al-Araf 189-190]

Now, if one is concerned that the problem could be related to Jinn or magic, one should do both the general protective measures, as well as the 7-day Ruqya program and the Ruqya bath. If one considers it necessary, one should then make the full Ruqya program.

One can also take blackcurrant oil or capsules, and read the following suras and verses on them, with the intention of Ruqya to destroy the magic:

Al-Fatihah; the three last Suras (3 Qul); Al-Baqarah 102; the verse of the throne (Al-Baqarah 255); Al-Baqarah 284-287;
Al-A'raf, 117-122; Yunus 79-82; Taha 65-69. (All these verses can be found in the appendix.)

Afterwards, blow on the oil / capsules and drink the normal dosage described on the pack until the pack is finished.

Treatment for general problems

Ruqya works not only with Jinn and magic related problems but also with normal medical problems.

Uthman ibn Abil رضي الله عنه *reported that he complained to the messenger of Allāh* ﷺ *about pain he had felt in his body since the time he became a Muslim. The Messenger of Allāh said to him, "Lay your hand upon the part of your body where you feel pain and say, 'Bismillah (in the name of Allāh) three times, then say seven times, A`udhu bi`izzat-illah wa qudratihi min sharri maajid wa uhadhir' (I seek refuge in the glory and power of Allāh before the evil of what I feel and worry about.)"* [32]

At-Tirmidhi added: He said, "I have done this, and Allāh has removed what I suffered, and I continued to make my family and others do the same."

---

[32] Muslim

Ruqya for children

When it comes to children, Ruqya is often easier than for adults, and the results can often be achieved more quickly. Ruqya cases in children can be divided into three categories:

1. Concern for children, without confirmed symptoms. This may involve medical problems that do not have a solution or a general feeling that the children have been plagued by the evil eye or that they are "not themselves." The full Ruqya program is less suitable for children at this stage. One can recommend the 7-day Ruqya Program, but without the honey for children less than one year old. The recitation can be done by the parents, and the program is usually well tolerated by people of all ages.

2. Confirmed symptoms, without a strong reaction from the child, and without the Jinn taking over. Symptoms can be the result of the treatment mentioned above, or when the child is displaying clear symptoms, but without a Jinn manifesting itself. For these children, the full Ruqya program is recommended, but the Ruqya can be performed in a very passive way. That means that the child doesn't have to sit like a statue, and there should be nothing that could scare the child, such as shouting. There is no need for the hijaamah to be applied either. For the majority of children, this treatment is enough to get rid of all symptoms, without any discomfort to the child, and without any of the usual Jinn-related antics.

3. Severe cases, in which the Jinn takes over the child, and the child becomes either extremely vocal or even violent. Once again, the full Ruqya program is

recommend, without hijaamah, but it may be necessary to be a little more active, keeping the child near, and pushing the Ruqya a little more.

At all times, the safety and well-being of the child is of paramount importance. The child is not an adult, so one should not treat it like one. The child should feel as comfortable with Ruqya as it possibly can. One should keep it relaxed and happy, and regularly check if they are OK. If necessary, play with them so they can relax. If you are a Raqi and are only coming for the Ruqya, then try to be around the child for a little while outside of the Ruqya session, to help them feel more comfortable with you.

NEVER hit a child! Hitting a Ruqya patient isn't a good idea at the best of times, and can lead to a rather long prison sentence, but hitting a child could cause them serious injury, and many children have died as a result of 'beating the Jinn'. All you have done in this case is to do the work of the shayṭān for them. If the Jinn is moving around in the body, a gentle massage of the affected area is more than enough. It will relax the child and put pressure on the Jinn. It is also very 'forgiving' in the sense that if you get the wrong place, it will not cause any harm to the child at all.

The hardest thing about Ruqya for children is that children are not able to explain their experiences and feelings like adults. They may naturally be fidgety and move around. This should not be misunderstood as a Jinn problem. Take time to observe the child, both inside and outside of the Ruqya, to establish a baseline, in terms of the behaviour of the child, and what might be considered abnormal.

If the child is old enough to understand, try to discuss with them, and most importantly, remove the fear of the shayṭān from them. Fear of the shayṭān can be much worse in children than adults, and we don't want the children scared to go to sleep. Make light of the issue, and tell them how weak the shayṭān is, and how he runs away from the Qur'an. Teach them simple things to say to protect themselves, like some of the things mentioned here.

When the Jinn speaks, one should try to bring him to Islam and convince him that he has to leave the body. (See chapter "Conversation with Jinn")

There isn't one best time to perform Ruqya, but if one notices the symptoms are bad at a certain time, such as after Maghrib, then one should do it when one feels the symptoms are strongest. Otherwise whenever it is most comfortable for the child.

One should be willing to change the time and the method, depending on progress. At the same time, one should not change too quickly, as this encourages the shayṭān to manipulate one.

Ruqya for non-Muslims

Allāh has made it clear that He has destined to unbelievers and those who do not remember Him, one (or more) devils who accompany them. And against the decree of Allāh one can't do anything! This is why most Raqis refuse treatment of non-Muslims. The Jinn can hide behind unbelief like behind a wall.

There are also Raqis who make the treatment on one condition: "When you get healed, you accept Islam!" Because the fact that someone asks for Ruqya signals that faith is already present to some extent.

I would join this view and advise non-Muslims the following:

➤ Follow the general protective measures against Jinn (see the corresponding chapter), e.g. clean your house from all pictures and statues, and use as much as possible things the Jinn do not like, such as black seed, honey, olive oil etc.

➤ Because non-Muslims are not allowed to touch the Qur'an in Arabic (because they are in the state of ritual impurity, as are Muslims who have not performed the prayer ablution), you should find someone who is willing to recite the Qur'an on you. If you have a Muslim friend who is willing to help, you should encourage him to follow as much as possible the 7-day program. If this is not possible, you should hear as much as possible Qur'an in audio form[33], which is a less good option, but one that should be mentioned.

---

[33] https://archive.org/details/Ar-RuqyaAs-shariahRecitationBySheikhAhmadAlAjmi /

> Taking a Ruqya bath, as explained earlier, but without reading the Qur'an, if you do not have a Muslim friend who can help.

All this may cause some relief.

The truth is that Islam the only thing is that can really help you. That is because the only true cure is to turn to the Creator of the heavens and the earth, and to submit to Him, to believe in Him and to accept His commandments and prohibitions.

There are many people from different religions who claim to be able to exorcise, but all of them use magic, and while it can sometimes cause a temporary effect and relief, it ends up getting worse than before.

I would therefore like to take this opportunity to invite you to Islam. You can read the story of how I came to Islam in my book "No Name Nomad"[34]. You can also contact me personally at habib@tauhid.net.

May Allāh heal you from all evil, and show you the right way.

---

https://www.youtube.com/watch?v=xQs1Bvbn9ww
[34] http://www.tauhid.net/nnn.html

The necessary patience

The key to Ruqya is patience and consistency. Many people say "it does not work!" For most of them, the problem is simply a lack of patience, specifically a lack of consistency and the false expectation that if they do the right thing, the problem should go away in a certain time.

If the doctor told you that you had cancer, you wouldn't come back after your first chemotherapy treatment and say, "Why am I not cured now?" That's because you would expect that it would take a year, perhaps two years to go into full remission and get the all clear.

This is a war between you and an army of the shayaateen. This war will be made up of many many battles, some of which you will win, and some of which you will lose. All of this has a wisdom in it that Allāh has chosen for you. The Prophet ﷺ fought his enemies for over 20 years until Allāh gave him victory over them, and yet he was the most complete of the people in faith, the one whose du'aa was answered, the one who was free of major sins, and the one whose past and future sins were forgiven. Despite this, Allāh chose to test him and the believers with over 20 years of battling their enemy before the people entered into Islam in crowds.

Allāh has told us in the Qur'an:

If a wound should touch you - there has already touched the [opposing] people a wound similar to it. And these days [of varying conditions] We alternate among the people so that Allah may make evident those who believe and [may] take to Himself from among you martyrs - and Allah does not like the wrongdoers. Or do you think of entering paradise without Allāh recognizing those who have fought among you and (without) recognizing the patient? [Ali Imran 139-142]

Allāh tests our faith with many things, but never does He impose on us an examination which we are not capable of bearing. And if we have patience, the trials will be good for us and will cleanse us.

"Whom Allâh wishes good, He tests him." [35]

"Truly, when Allāh loves people, He lets them go through trials. Whoever is content with it, for him is contentment, and he who becomes angry, for him is anger." [36]

Furthermore, it may be that the weapon is perfect, but the arm which holds the weapon is weak, or the arm is strong but the aim is poor. It is only when the weapon is good, and the arm that wields it is strong, and the aim of the person is accurate that the weapon can be used to its true effect. For this reason, you should be self-critical and should be asking yourself if your sins are the reason why the help of Allāh is delayed, and you should be pushing yourself to constantly improve. This self-reflection and self-criticism is healthy up to a certain point, but it's not healthy when it causes you to reach the level where you despair of the help of Allāh.

Go, O my sons, and ascertain concerning Joseph and his brother, and despair not of the Mercy of Allah. Lo! none despaireth of the Mercy of Allah save disbelieving folk. [Yusuf 87]

---

[35] Buchari
[36] Tirmidhi

Make sure that you are either doing everything that is recommended, or exceeding it, and then be patient, and expect that the help of Allāh will come.

Ruqya can only be judged as successful if the patient does not show any further symptoms and has been blessed with a complete relief from the problem. This is something that usually happens in phases, and each phase has its own challenges. In a sense, the last stage of the treatment, if the patient feels better, is one of the most important times and one in which people make the most mistakes. There are some important points to consider when approaching the end of treatment:

1. Do not stop Ruqya. This is the #1 mistake that we see people make. One Jinn leaves, and so the person feels so much better that they stop treatment. One complete month of Ruqya is recommend, at the same intensity as before, until one can comfortable say that the person is genuinely better. This will preserve one - with the grace of Allāh - from many errors, thinking the patient is better, but something remains. This can either be because the Jinn are fooling you into thinking that they have gone, or because one Jinn has left and another, who was latent, becomes active. It also catches cases of the Jinn returning to the person after leaving, and cases where the person has been afflicted with something, such as the evil eye, leading to Jinn possession, in which the Jinn leaves, but the effects of the prior affliction remain. Note that the Raqi does not necessarily have to read for this period, but the patient and/or family members can read, and the Raqi can keep an eye on things, from time to time.

2. Don't accept 90%. This is closely related to the point made above. A lot of people get to 90% better, then

stop, because they think that is good enough. The affliction then has the chance to grow and flourish again. If you had cancer, you would not be content to stop with 90% of the malignant cancer removed, because you know that the 10% has the potential to grow again. Likewise, you should not be content with 90% of the affliction gone - aim for 100%.

3. Different phases mean different modes of attack for the shayṭān to take advantage of. If one door closes for the shayṭān, he will simply move on to another method. So, it might be that the shaking and the fitting stops, but the whispering and the confusion increases. Then, the whispering stops, but laziness in the prayer kicks in. The key to successful treatment is remaining constant and patient in tackling the problem, and continuing to adapt to the changes that are happening. One one hand, this requires consistency: don't stop the Ruqya program, no matter what happens. On the other hand, it requires adding specific things to deal with specific challenges. For example, adding the treatment against waswasah, in order to deal specifically with the whispering, while not stopping the usual Ruqya program.

4. Once the problem is gone, the person remains vulnerable. This is like a medical patient who has just undergone major surgery. Upon successful completion of the procedure, he remains vulnerable to illness and infection. This is also true of people who have completed Ruqya; they remain vulnerable. For this reason, even when the Ruqya stops, the person must be extremely observant in protecting themselves from further problems. Finally, they should be willing to resume their treatment at the first sign of a relapse.

5.   It may even be that it is better if the problem persists, but only if one has the necessary patience:

Atha bin Rabah رضي الله عنه *reported Abdullah bin Abbas* رضي الله عنه, *who pointed to a black woman who was promised paradise (Ummu Zuffar). He said that the woman once came to the Prophet* ﷺ *and said, "I am suffering from the disease Ayan (epileptic seizures), and every time I get cramps, I lose consciousness, sometimes people seeing my nakedness. Pray to Allāh, that I may be healed." The Messenger of Allāh* ﷺ *said, "If you will be patient, you will come to paradise. If you want to be cured, I will pray to Allāh." The woman replied, "I will have patience. But pray that I will not be naked when I lose my consciousness." And the Messenger of Allāh* ﷺ *prayed for her.* [37]

Faith and patience are the keys to paradise, and whoever has patience will have success.

… and the patient in tribulation and adversity and time of war. Such are they who are sincere. Such are the God-fearing. [Al-Baqarah 177]

O ye who believe! Endure, outdo all others in endurance, be ready, and observe your duty to Allah, in order that ye may succeed. [Ali Imran 200]

---

[37] [Bukhâri 5652]

Treatment

by a Raqi

The Healer

The healer should have a good character and an exemplary way of life. In order to heal, he needs *ikhlas* (sincerity), the right *aqidah* (doctrine of faith), must follow the model of the Prophet, must be God-fearing, be constant in worship, keep away from forbidden things, have experience, be constant in God-remembrance and have patience. His prayers should already have been answered by Allāh in some difficult situations, showing that this person is accepted by Allāh, and that he has a certain strenght in faith, for the stronger the faith of the Raqi, the more effective the healing.

The healer should try as much as possible to be only a mediator and concentrate on the Koran, and to let Allāh do the work. That is, he focuses on the recitation of the Koran, until he feels how Allāh Himself addresses evil with His word. Imagine how Allāh hates sorcery and evil-doing Jinn, and try to hate what Allāh hates.

The healer should have an understanding of different types of mental disorders and common diseases to make a correct diagnosis. If he can not properly diagnose the presence of 'Ain, Jinn or Magic, other trustworthy professionals should be consulted.

The profession of Raqi - a vocation

There are some people who know about Ruqya, but few who practice it professionally. The requirements are enourmous: Desperate people and occasionally "cracked characters", are knocking at one's door at any time of the day and night. Devils are constantly struggling to attack the healer and his family. Sorcerers try to avenge themselves because the Raqi destroyed their magic, or who just want to test just how good the Raqi is already.

In addition, the Raqi has to strive not to develop *riya* (show-off), once he has success and people come in crowds, and to keep his intentions pure for Allāh alone, and not to reap praise and adoration, or to make a lot of money when he realizes that many people are willing to pay big sums for getting healed!

Normally, no one is choosing to become a Raqi. Allāh is choosing them and imposes on them difficult lessons and hard tests. Often, Raqis were themselves victims of witchcraft, or their family members had problems, and so they were forced to learn about Ruqya, and they met other healers where they gained experience.

I am not talking about those who are doing Ruqya purely for business or "occasional Raqis" (as myself). I speak of those whom Allāh has called for this profession: They are usually the best of the Ummah! The daily confrontation with the devils let them reach levels of God-reliance, God-fearingness, and God-remembrance, which are hardly attainable for the average Muslim.

Because devils hate the Sunnah, the Raqis often are the ones who practice the Sunnah most sincere. They are also the ones who keep aloof from sectarianism and debates because they know that this is all from Satan.

For the devils, only the personal qualities of the Raqi are important. Allāh helps His humble servants and not the arrogant who always believe they know better and deem themselves among the rightly guided group.

One will find that the best Raqis (or rather those whose Ruqya is blessed by Allāh) are those who appear quite insignificant or even contemptible in the eyes of ordinary people. But when the devils see them, they immediately get frightened so that patients (or rather the Jinn in them) often scream and want to run away when they have just seen the Raqi.

It is reported[38] that Ahmad bin Hanbal, the founder of the Hanbali School of Jurisprudence, once sat in the mosque when an acquaintance came in and told that a Jinn had went into Jariyah, the servant of the caliph. Ahmad bin Hanbal prayed to Allāh, then gave one of his sandals to the acquaintance and told him to take it and to show it to the servant (or rather the Jinn in her) and say, "Get out of Jariyah, or Imam Ahmad will hit you 70 times (with this sandal)", whereupon the Jinn immediately left the body of the servant.

Does one want to accuse Imam Ahmad now of having commited *bid'ah* (innovation) because Rasulallāh ﷺ and the Salaf did not use sandals for Ruqya? In Ruqya, only the true qualities of the Raqi count, and precisely these qualities do count on the Last Day too!

In Granada, the Imam of the mosque in the Albaycin once said to a new convert who was somewhat confused because of all the various groups in Islam: "Do not worry about what the Muslims disagree about. Worry about what they agree on!" That was a very wise piece of advice!

All Muslims know that it is a duty to pray five times, to fast, and to keep away from sins etc! And that Allāh asks us to be united and not to split into groups[39]. Therefore, the Ruqya is also accepted from those who keep far from the debates.

---

[38] In Thabaqat Al Hanabilah by Ibnu Abi Ya'la
[39] Ali Imran 103

It is a big plus when the Raqi is also familiar with prophetic medicine, especially *hijamah* (cupping), since Jinn are normally in the bloodstream and where the polluted blood accumulates, which is why they often get sucked out with the blood.

Just as one should keep one's environment and oneself externally clean, one should keep oneself inwardly clean too, e.g. by hijamah, fasting or sweating. This also weakens the Jinn. Therefore, if one notices that the house of the Raqi is not clean, one may leave straight away, let alone if the Raqi himself is dirty or smoking cigarettes.

Sins of all kinds on the side of the Raqi greatly weaken the effect of the Ruqya and offer the Jinn opportunity to avenge itself. For example, if the Raqi looks at a woman with desire, the Jinn may appear in the dream as a beautiful woman, and beacuse the defense is weakened by sin, the Jinn can harm him. Consequently, a Raqi can allow himself hardly any transgressions, which of course is an excellent training for him but also a very strenuous one.

The Raqi has to prepare himself against being occasionally attacked by sorcerers when they see that their magic got destroyed. The Raqi should therefore often treat oneself, the family and also the house, and quickly recognize when something is wrong. InshaAllāh Allāh will guard him and send angels to protect him. But, especially as a beginner, one should draw a line and not load up things on one's back that are too heavy. One should not sacrifice the well-being of one's own family for others and bring one's own life out of balance. This also means that one should not get too emotionally involved and not suffer for others, but only try to help them.

In general, a Raqi must comply with a strict program of Dhikr, but especially after each Ruqya. It is advised to take a Ruqya bath regularly. For those who only occasionally exercise Ruqya, it is sufficient to recite the verse of the throne seven times after each canonical prayer for three days.

The Prophet ﷺ has not protested that the Companions have received a wage for Ruqya; on the contrary, he has asked for a share. People must understand that a Raqi, who works professionally, invests a lot, and that it is only fair if he is paid for his efforts. The patient must also be made aware that healing comes only from Allāh and therefore can not be guaranteed.

As a beginner one should let the people decide how much they want to pay. When becoming more professional, however, one should set fair tariffs for the time invested, but never refuse to treat people who aren't able to pay.

Raqis should organize themselves in their country of residence, share their healing methods and take note of their successes, but also their failures. The more one can prove that Ruqya often helps with problems in which Western medicine has failed, the better the image of Ruqya and thus also of Islam itself.

The Healing

The healer should inform himself well about the complaints and be able to make a diagnosis. In the course of the anamnesis, the patient's history of his previous complaints is analyzed. The result of the anamnesis allows to draw conclusions about the life situation and causal connections, in order ultimately to decide whether the application of Ruqya is advisable in this case. Like any illness, a disease caused by magic or Jinn has its symptoms, which can be used to determine whether a person is affected or not (see also "Diagnosis by Koran recitation" in the following chapter).

It is important that one is able to tell if it is a pure attack by Jinn or if magic is involved, because one should not attack the Jinn before the magic has not been removed.

The Raqi should ask the patient a few important questions, depending on the situation and the relationship:

➢   What does he do in life?

➢   If he is looking for a job, for how long already?

➢   No problems with work or studies?

➢   Are the relationships with others in order?

➢   Ask about the family. If he is not married, but old enough for it, ask him why not yet.

➢   If he is married, ask if everything is going well (also in bed, provided this questions does not pose complications). If there are signs of problems, ask what exactly the difficulties are. Is he healthy? In case of a problem, what is the origin? And what is the medical diagnosis?

➢ Ask if the patient has problems with digestion, pain in the ovaries, difficulties with the period, headache, back pain, heaviness in arms or legs, or skin problems such as spots or eczema.

➢ Does the patient sleep well, does he wake up feeling refreshed or tired? Does he have nightmares?

➢ Does the patient suspect someone has bewitched him?

➢ Has he ever used a talisman or a magician for treatment? If so, he must regret this and have the sincere intention to never do this again. If the magician or "healer" has given him anything, for example, to bury it next to the house, this must first be destroyed. (See the appendix: How to destroy a Buhul?)

➢ Has he ever learned martial arts such as Pencak Silat or Kung-Fu? If so, has he ever participated in rituals to promote "inner strength"? Here, too, he has to repent and have the intention to dissociate himself from it in the future. He must also agree that this "inner strength" is destroyed by Ruqya.

➢ Has he ever participated in rituals which include bid'ah like extreme forms of "Dhikr"?

➢ The healer should educate the patient about why Jinn enter a body and what to do about it.

➢ The healer should remind the patient that no misfortune occurs without the permission of Allāh, and that if he has patience, the discomfort will be good for him.

The place for the Ruqya should be clean and quiet, may not have any pictures and far from music, car noise, TV and other disturbances. It is best in a mosque. It is recommended to read the verse of the throne with the intention of protecting the place from external attacks and to supplicate Allāh accordingly.

Both healers and patients should be in the state of ritual purity. The patient should regret any sins, recite *Istighfar*, and ask the help of Allāh. The healer should make the patient feel relaxed, and let him leave negative feelings like disappointment, anger, despair, and the like.

In more serious cases, the healer should pray 2 or 4 Rakaat Shalat Mutlaq and ask the help of Allāh. Then he recites Ta'awudz, Basmallāh, Istighfar, Salawat, al-Fatihah, Ayat al-Kursi, Al-Ikhlas, Al-Falaq and An-Nas, blows into his hands and rubs his whole body with the intention of making this a protection from the Jinn in order that Jinn leaving the patient's body do not directly attack the healer himself. Then he should take the intention to practice Ruqya and to use Qur'anic verses as weapons against the Jinn or magic, to heal with the Qur'an and, if necessary, to send the magic back to the sorcerer.

The patient should listen attentively to the recitation of the Qur'an, and also order the Jinn mentally to listen to the recitation of the Qur'an.

There are a number of individual techniques, and here, as with the rest of medicine too, applies the motto: "He who heals is right", as long as no unlawful methods are used. Only seek out healers who use the Qur'an and apply certain traditional techniques, such as placing the hand on the affected body parts, (light) hitting on the back, rubbing, knocking, blowing, or reciting on water with Qur'anic verses.

It is impossible for an unbeliever to understand how certainty of faith, intention and visualization, together with the power of the Qur'an, can have such an effect on the physical plane, and even Muslims who see it for the first time will be astonished, if not shocked!

Caution Dukun!

Never visit for treatment a "Dukun" (shaman, medicine man, magician), who probably can expel the Jinn, but who works with the help of Jinn himself. Not only does it become worse afterwards, one can also commit shirk. A dukun can be recognised, among other things, as follows:

He asks the name of the patient and the name of the mother.

He asks for a personal belonging of the patient.

He sometimes asks for an animal with certain criteria that gets sacrificed without pronouncing the name of Allāhs and then thrown or buried somewhere.

He writes some incomprehensible letters on a piece of paper, sometimes even the Qur'an in a strange form, e.g. circular shape. The paper is then to be hung over the door, buried next to the house, or to be dissolved in water and to drink. It is intended to protect or bring special blessings. Or he gives another object to be buried at the house.

Murmurs some incomprehensible mantras.

Invites the patient to stay in a dark room for a certain time.

Orders the patient not to touch any water for a certain time.

> *Gives one a paper that he wants you to burn and which generates smoke.*
>
> *Gives strange things to eat, e.g. intestines.*
>
> *Or he even wants to have sex with the patient.*

The healer (if he is a man) is only allowed to practice Ruqya in the presence of a family member if the patient is a woman (except in emergencies, and then not alone) and should not touch the woman if possible. If he must, he must wear gloves. (There are different opinions about this, just like with a doctor of the opposite sex, too.)

One usually begins to recite al-Fatihah clearly, while the patient sits in the direction of the kiblat (prayer direction). There are also Raqis who recommend that the patient is lying down to relax better, and his entire body is covered with a sheet, or at least the eyes to better be able to concentrate on listening to the Qur'an. Thereafter, other verses and suras are recited (see Appendix).

The healer adjusts the recitation with the reaction of the patient or the Jinn and follows his intuition. Should a good reaction follow after reciting al-Fatihah and Ayatul-Kursi, one can proceed with just these verses. A reaction can happen very quickly, even before the healer has started with Ruqya yet. But it can also take hours, when there are many "shields" (spiritual walls, which the healer has to break through). The reactions are also very different. There can be no or a barely perceptible reaction. There may be vehement reactions during which the patient dances, does movements like practicing Tai-Chi, starts singing and claps his hands, attacks the healer, cries fervidly or does other things. Quite entertaining for spectators!

Under normal circumstances, the patient will get warm after a few minutes, may have to vomit (which is why plastic bags should be kept ready), and he may lose consciousness. He does not fall asleep though, but the Jinn "takes over" the patient's body. He will often try to keep his ears shut in order not to hear the Qur'an. He will look at one with angry eyes, but look more and more tormented after a while and will begin groaning. This is the time when one can start talking to the Jinn (see chapter "Conversation with Jinn").

As a "newbie" one will be astonished about the different characters there are among the Jinn, as with humans. If the Jinn is female, she will speak with a female voice, which sounds quite strange from the mouth of a male patient, just as vice versa. One can ask the Jinn for his name, whether he is a believer (which is usually not the case), how many other Jinn are still in the patient's body, and why he has entered the patient's body. One should exhort the Jinn and remind him of the punishment of Allāh if he does not repent. He should be asked to become a Muslim.

Often one does not get a reaction and only a sarcastic, arrogant laughter, but this usually fades away quickly when one continues to recite Qur'an and starts with other techniques such as light strokes on the back and supplicating to Allāh to let the fist turn into an iron hammer in the subtle world. Or one may tingle the patient with one's finger and ask Allāh to let the finger become a glowing thorn in the subtle world. This may sound funny, and many will consider this to be humbug until they have seen it themselves how spirituality and visualization have a direct effect on the physical plane.

Only very strong Jinn will still maintain their arrogance during such a treatment. This is the time to ask them again why they are in the body, where the Buhul is hidden, to persuade them to become Muslim, and to ask them to leave the body of the patient when they do not want to get destroyed.

It may happen that one has to deal with a thousand-year old Ifrit, who remains arrogant even then and says, "Yes, the verse of the throne, I already know" and begins to recite it himself (but probably not to the end). As a beginner, one will have a hard time then! Remember, however, that all power is with Allāh, and that the Jinn has literally crossed the limit by occupying a human body and has become vulnerable. Even the biggest white shark on land is at the mercy of a small person. No one can resist the word of Allâh! It only takes more time and patience, and perhaps more Tazkiyah (purification) on the side of the patient and possibly also on the side of the healer. Sometimes it can take weeks before a strong Jinn finally withdraws. A Jinn will remain in the body until the pain that he suffers is greater than the desire to remain in the body, and this is again depending on why the Jinn has intruded the body in the first place and how strong he is.

If the Jinn is ready to accept Islam, one says the shahadah (confession of faith). Once the Jinn has repeated the shahadah he has to swear that he leaves the body now and does not return any more and does not occupy any other human body again.

In the case of a Jinn being in the body because an ancestor of the patient has made a pact with Jinn, this pact has to be dissolved and the pact has to be declared invalid. Then the Jinn is asked to leave the body. If he does, the patient's body will suddenly slacken, and he will regain consciousness.

It may well be that the Jinn has only pretended conversion to Islam in order to escape the pain. Jinn can be hardly trusted anyway! Then it is time to exhort him one last time and tell him that if he does not leave the body, he will be destroyed now with the permission of God.

Which technique is now being used depends, among other things, on where the Jinn stays in the body. In a technique one imagines, the edge of the hand would be a sword, with which the throat of the Jinn is cut. Or one gives him poison to drink, e.g. Ruqya water. Or one burns him with the verses of the Qur'an. Sometimes the Jinn will still try to fight back and attack the healer. But the movements are generally weak and not well coordinated. One can, for example, take a prayer rug and hit the patient's back with it while imagining it would be an iron hammer in the subtle world. It is also possible to ask God to let the Jinn stick to the floor, or that his hands get tied.

There are several techniques to investigate whether the Jinn went already completely out of the body. Often, several sessions are required until all the Jinn are out, also depending on the extent to which sorcery is involved and how much effort the patient is making himself.

Diagnosis by recitation of the Koran

The patient's response to the recitation of the Qur'an can help with the diagnosis.

- o The most typical reaction if there is magic will be heat all over the body: the magic is burning.

- o The person can feel something going out of him: the magic leaves him.

- o If the person feels heavy or gets goose bumps, does not want to hear the Qur'an, gets drowsiness or becomes nervous: this is a sign that Jinn are in the body.

- o The person relaxes or calms down, or even falls asleep: this can mean three things: either he has been given magic to make him nervous and the Koran reduces the effect of the magic so that the person relaxes; or the magic causes him to be constantly tired even when he has slept enough. The effect diminishes during Koran recitation and he falls into a restful sleep. Or the Jinn lets the patient fall asleep, so he does not hear the Koran.

- o If the person moves or speaks without his will: We have Jinn.

- o Headaches can mean different things: there are Jinn in or outside the body; magic set in the head, or hanged-up magic that goes into the head.

- o A combination of reactions indicates a combination of problems. After the recitation, the patient is usually tired and exhausted.

- o No or little reaction: The person has only a minor or no problem, or the Jinn is outside the body and controls the patient from the outside. In this case, a simple recitation is enough to burn the connection and disconnect the Jinn with the person.

A diagnosis of Jinn or magic does not exclude the other. When one perceives clear symptoms in the patient's life, his body, his mental condition, and his dreams, one can also conclude a diagnosis without a reaction.

Many people, however, attribute many things to the influence of magic, where there are quite normal causes, perhaps because their daughter has fallen in love with a non-Muslim. Others may even ask to use "white magic", e.g. to get the wife back who left them, and are not aware of the fact that there is no such thing as "white magic", but generally an act that excludes one from Islam. In order to get more blessings in life, there is only one way: faith, taqwa, good deeds, and keeping away from sins.

Different treatment techniques

The following techniques are mostly based on reports of the Prophet ﷺ and have been tested and partially further developed by Raqis. Before using these techniques, one must follow the initial procedures, as described in the chapter "The Healing".

Laying on hands

> *Uthman ibn Abil* رضي الله عنه *reported that he complained to the messenger of Allāh ﷺ about pain he had felt in his body since the time he became a Muslim. The Messenger of Allāh ﷺ said to him, "Lay your hand upon the part of your body where you feel pain and say, 'Bismillah (in the name of Allāhs) three times, then say seven times: ,A`udhu bi`izzat-illah wa qudratihi min sharri maajid wa uhadhir' (I seek refuge in the glory and power of Allāh from the evil of what I feel and worry about.)"*[40]

Place the hand on the affected spot for 3-5 minutes and recite verses from the Koran, especially those listed in the appendix or as far as they are memorized, and see the patient's reaction.

If a reaction on part of the patient occurs, such as crying, groaning, trembling, or burping, recitation should be continued until the patient vomits. Or try beating the affected spots or the back, and order the Jinn to leave the body, for example, by saying: "*Ukhruj ya AduwAllāh*" (Out with you, enemy of Allāh).

---

[40] Muslim

If no exact point of pain can be localized, place the hand on the apex of the head and recite, among other verses, Sura Hud 56:

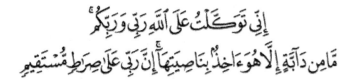

Inni tawakaltu 'alAllāhi rabbi wa rabbikum maa min daabbatin illa huwa achisun binaa shiyatihaa. Inna rabbi 'ala shiraathim-mustaqiem.

Lo! I have put my trust in Allah, my Lord and your Lord. Not an animal but He doth grasp it by the forelock! Lo! my Lord is on a straight path.

Knocking / beating

Knocking or beating is the technique commonly used when when there was already a reaction after reciting Ruqya verses. The goal is to expel the Jinn from the body, as the Messenger of Allāh ﷺ has done, reported in several ahadeeth, like the one by Mathar bin Abdurrahman Al-A'naq, who tells of a mentally ill girl who was taken to the Prophet ﷺ. After her bonds were loosened and she sat with her back to the Prophet ﷺ, the Prophet ﷺ hit her back while he said several times: "*Ukhruj ya AduwAllāh*" (Out with you, enemy of Allāh). Then he prayed and rubbed his hands over his face, and the girl was cured. [41]

Instead of hitting the back, one can also knock rhythmically on the head (not too hard, of course), or on the shoulders or chest, as reported by the Prophet ﷺ, when he treated Uthman Abi Ash رضي الله عنه , who often forgot the number of rakaat in prayer. [42]

---

[41] Thabrani in al-Haitsami, Majma'uz Zawa'id 9/3
[42] Ibn Majah

Applying pressure

This technique[43] exerts pressure by pressing the fingers on affected points while quoting Ruqya verses. This technique is also suitable for locating the site where the Jinn is hiding by pressing along the blood channels, and on the spots commonly used for cupping (hijamah). One can also press along the spine.

Should a reaction occur, e.g. that the patient groans or screeches when one touches certain spots, one should ensure that it is the Jinn in the patient who feels the pain and not the patient himself. One makes sure the patient is awake by letting him recite Istighfar and talking to him. If the patient is not conscious or semi-conscious, one knows that this is the spot where the Jinn resides.

To prevent the Jinn from moving and hiding in another place, recite Sura Yasin, verse 9, with the intention of blocking the Jinn. Then blow on the index finger and the middle finger and describe with them a circle around the affected spot (counterclockwise).

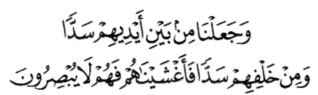

Wa ja'alnaa min baini aidiehim saddan wa min chalfihim saddan fa-aghshainaahum fahum la yubshiruun.

And We have erected a wall before them, and have built a wall behind them, and We have concealed them, so that they can not see.

Then use other techniques to expel or eliminate the Jinn.

---

[43] Reported by Aisha r.a. and Sufyan bin 'Uyainah r.a.

Brushing

This technique is suitable to relieve pain as reported by Aisha رضي الله عنه when Rasulallāh ﷺ lay on his deathbed and recited the Mu'awidhatan (the two last Suras of the Qur'an), then blew on his hands and rubbed with them his body. When he was too weak to do so, Aisha رضي الله عنه did it for him. [44]

But the technique is also suitable for healing, as reported by Ibn Abbas رضي الله عنه, when a woman brought her sick child to the Prophet ﷺ and and told him it was mad (possessed). The Prophet ﷺ recited Qur'an and Du'a, then brushed the child's breast, whereupon the child vomited and a little creature came out of its mouth.

Normally one tries to expel the disease or the Jinn by brushing towards the mouth, e.g. along the spine or from the abdomen upwards.

Blowing

This technique was often used by the Prophet ﷺ, both with a little spit and without. One recites Ruqya verses and then blows vigorously on the affected spots with the intention to burn and destroy the spell or the Jinn, and to heal the patient.

Visualization

During visualization one asks Allāh for example to let one's finger be a glowing thorn in the subtle world with which one can torture the Jinn. Or one asks Allāh to let the edge of the hand become a sword, the fist an iron hammer, the water to be poison and so on.

---

[44] Buchari, Muslim

As the Prophet ﷺ said, everything depends on the intention, and in the subtle world this has drastic effects.

Treatment with candles

A very effective method is to use candles during recitation. When the patient is lying on his back, candles are placed at his naked soles, which have been previously recited on, preferably two for each foot. The patient should see that the candles are not so close to the foot that they can cause pain or even burn, so that he knows that during the subsequent recitation of the Qur'an, during which the Jinn "wakes up", it is the Jinn that suffers, but transmits some pain to the patient, so that the patient suffers from the heat as well. This will hopefully help the patient to withstand the pain because he knows that it is not actually him being burned, but the Jinn.

The killing in the dream

One can kill Jinn, and possibly sorcerers and those who have ordered the magic, in one's sleep. Before going to sleep, one recites the verse of the throne 11 times and then the second part of al-Baqarah 148 minimum 11 times, but better 30, 50 or even 100 times:

$$\text{أَيْنَ مَا تَكُونُوا يَأْتِ بِكُمُ ٱللَّهُ جَمِيعًا ۚ إِنَّ ٱللَّهَ عَلَىٰ كُلِّ شَىْءٍ قَدِيرٌ}$$

Aina maa takunuu ya'tibikumullahu jamie'aan. InnAllāha 'ala kulli schain qadier.

Wherever you are, Allāh will bring you together. Truly, Allāh has power over all things.

Before falling asleep, one must make the intention of reciting the Qur'an on all one encounters in a dream and to kill one's enemies, whoever they may be, and to ask Allāh to help one. When one does this, the person or entity one meets in the dream will try to flee. One has to chase it until one catches it, and then read the Qur'an, preferably the verse of the throne, or something that one remembers easily, until one kills it. One can catch the person or the being by grasping it with the hand in the dream, or with the eyes, for as long as one looks at it, it can not disappear. When it tries to flee, one recites the second part of Baqarah 148, and one will be able to easily catch it inshaAllah.

Should the Jinn press on one, and one feels weight on one and is paralyzed, do not panic! Do not fight with the Jinn, just grab it, recite the verse of the throne in your head until the tongue is free, and then continue to recite the Qur'an until the Jinn is dead.

One should not be surprised if one hears in the next few days of the death of the person suspected of sorcery.

Conversation with Jinn

There are Raqis who do not spend much time talking to Jinn because they perceive it as a waste of time. They ask the Jinn to leave the body if he does not want to be killed, and call the Jinn an enemy of Allāh. This puts the Jinn into the defensive, and naturally he will start to lie.

But when one talks to the Jinn, it is an opportunity to improve the situation. Often the Jinn has not entered the patient's body by his own will, but has been forced to do so. Perhaps he did not like his mission, or perhaps he was threatened that his family would be taken as a hostage if he does not carry out the mission. Or he does not understand magic and how he himself has come into the body. Perhaps he can not leave the body because the magic binds him.

For this reason, one should not look at the Jinn as an enemy, but try to cooperate with them, which considerably increases the chances of finding the true reason why the Jinn is there, and perhaps also the Buhul. The Jinn can help destroy the magic and is freed himself.

One must also understand that Jinn can be hurt by humans, and even be mutilated, and that they, as an emotional being, want to practice revenge, sometimes for years because they do not have much else to do, and that man offers the Jinn food and accommodation. This should also be taken into account during a conversation.

A Jinn, who falls in love with a man, does not think much about entering the body. In their world, the Jinn form a couple, without any ceremonies, and it believes that it can do that with humans too. The Jinn usually does not understand that occupying a human body is wrong. On the contrary, it will often see the rival as illegal, ie the wife or the husband of the person concerned.

Why is the Jinn there?

This is the most important thing to know. One can ask him, "What are you doing here?" Often he will not answer, for his power comes from the fact that he is invisible and hidden from us. The more they are discovered, the more we know about them and the more they are weakened. That is why they are suspicious and afraid, we use the information we receive against them.

One has to ask further to get an answer: "Have you been sent by a sorcerer? Has anyone made you come? "Or," Did he hurt you, did he deserve punishment?" Or: "Do you love him? Do you want to be alone with him?"

One has to ask questions until one has answers. Maybe the Jinn will lie, but it will not be hard to see. The Jinn is always lying for a reason. For example, for to stop you reading Qur'an, he will speak through the patient's mouth and promise to go or become a Muslim. In this case, one should not bother him, but ask the purpose of his presence.

To check if the Jinn is lying, one has to cross-examine and quickly ask questions, so that the Jinn does not have much time to think and is possibly entangled in contradictions. Jinn can not lie well.

One can ask him, "How did it happen? Where was it? Since when? What kind of sorcery is it (if it is sorcery)?" Then we check whether the answers are plausible. Of course, we do not have to believe him, and also Jinn can make mistakes. The goal is simply to find a solution, and we can add the testimony of the Jinn to the diagnosis. If he says, for example, the magic would have been eaten while we believe it would be in a cemetery, we treat for both cases.

However, the Jinn often fear us because they know that they get burned. To talk with them about magic and to get useful answers, one has to soothe them by saying, "Do not be afraid, I will not hurt you! I just want to undo the spell so that you are free and the person is healed. I just want you to help me destroy the spell."

If the Jinn is tied to sorcery, it is important to define the kind of sorcery: eaten, written, placed in the body or stepped upon. It may be that the Jinn knows nothing about magic and is not able to give information, but mostly he knows it.

If he does not know, one can ask him, "Can you look into the belly, whether there is any magic?" Or, "Is there anything that keeps you from going out?" Or simply: "Where is the magic hidden?"

Then ask the Jinn whether he is bound to the magic or not, whether the patient still has other magic and whether there are other Jinn. Ask how the other magic is made and why the other Jinn are present.

It may happen that the Jinn refuses to speak, although he has the ability to do so. Pity! Apply the treatment!

But one can also meet very talkative Jinn; they will talk hours and hours as long as one is ready to listen to them. The healer has to master the situation and know when the Jinn is chattering uselessly and interrupting him by saying, "We just want to treat him. We just want to know what is necessary. "

If there are other important information, e.g. about whether other people in the family are affected, take the time to listen, but stop him when he starts chattering again.

One should not ask the Jinn about the person who sent the spell. It is impossible to take revenge on sorceres except by prayers, and when they know they have been discovered, they can begin again. It is best to show them no change in behavior so they think their magic works. If one knows who the sorcerer is, one surely would change one's attitude towards him and he becomes aware of it. The Jinn can also confuse the person or simply lie, and then the wrong person is blamed.

If one has to know who the sorcerer is to avoid him, make prayer and ask Allāh to show one the person and tell one how to protect oneself. The best thing is to use the invocation of the oppressed, which is most accepted by Allāh (see also the chapter "Returning the Spell"). Sorcerers do not deserve pity or forgiveness. So ask Allāh to punish them and avenge you. Do not forget to have the intention to send the magic back to the sender when reciting the Qur'an.

Who is the Jinn?

It is not curiosity to ask for its name, gender, age, and religion, and how long it is already in the body, but it prepares the next steps. Jinn feel strong and arrogant when people do not know them and fear them. When they are made to reveal their identity, they discard their arrogance and open up.

One also has to ask the Jinn how it enters the body of the person, its exact position and its effect on the patient. All this will help one to verify the truth of its words, but it is also a valuable piece of information to drive it out of the patient if the subsequent negotiations are unsuccessful.

Then one can put cupping glasses at the spot where it sits and where it enters.

By informing it about our intentions and asking for its help, it developed kindness and began to trust us. It is therefore predisposed to accept our sermon.

Suggest him to become a Muslim

If the Jinn is already Muslim, one will skip this step, of course. It is not surprising how many Muslim Jinn work for sorcerers, revenge on people, or see humans as lovers. They are just like most human Muslims too, full of ignorance and sins.

If the Jinn is a Muslim, one must speak of prayer and good deeds. The religious practices of Jinn differ from ours, but there are more similarities than differences. One can tell it that it can learn about Islamic practices with Muslim Jinn in mosques or directly in Mecca.

Non-Muslim Jinn can be preached in two steps: The Jinn must first realize that Islam is the truth. The second step is to make him convert.

One should not begin to ask him to become a Muslim, because that would be like asking a stranger to become a Muslim. One does not know his present faith or knowledge of Islam. It is therefore very unlikely that he will respond to this request. In addition, such an introduction could affect the rest of the discussion. Before he is asked to become a Muslim, make sure that he has recognized the truth of Islam. One starts a discussion without rushing.

Some Jinn do not want to name their religion or discuss it. Nevertheless, try to make the Jinn speak. If he does not answer the question "What is your religion?" one should ask: "Are you Muslim, Christian, Jewish or atheist?" "You have no religion?"

If he does not answer, one can say, "Do you not want to tell your religion?" When he replies, "No," one can ask, "Why not?" and try to get a discussion started. Try to guess the reason for his rejection and provoke him, such as "You do not want to name your religion because you know it is wrong!" Or, "You know you're going to be a Muslim when you talk to us, so that's why you're silent!"

When he says, "Yes," one asks immediately, "If you know your religion is wrong, is there any reason to hang on to it?" Or, "If you know you'll be convinced, is there any reason for you to refuse to become a Muslim?"

Do not use scientific or rational arguments, but ask him if he knows what the Qur'an is. If he does not know, or knows it, but does not realize that it is Allāh's book, tell him: "To prove His existence, Allāh sends prophets with miracles. The miracle of the last Prophet Muhammad, blessings and peace be upon him, is the Qur'an. It is a miracle for people and Jinn. Its linguistic and scientific content is a miracle for people. It is a miracle for you, as it burns Jinn, if they are disbelieving or disobedient. I will read the Qur'an, so that you can examine it yourself." Then read Sura ar-Rahman verses 33-35:

يَٰمَعْشَرَ ٱلْجِنِّ وَٱلْإِنسِ إِنِ ٱسْتَطَعْتُمْ أَن تَنفُذُواْ مِنْ أَقْطَارِ ٱلسَّمَٰوَٰتِ وَٱلْأَرْضِ فَٱنفُذُواْ لَا تَنفُذُونَ إِلَّا بِسُلْطَٰنٍ ۝ فَبِأَيِّ ءَالَآءِ رَبِّكُمَا تُكَذِّبَانِ ۝ يُرْسَلُ عَلَيْكُمَا شُوَاظٌ مِّن نَّارٍ وَنُحَاسٌ فَلَا تَنتَصِرَانِ ۝

Yaa m'aschral Jinni wal imi inistata'tum an tanfusuu min aqthaaris-samawaati wal ardhi fanfusuu. La tanfusuuna illa bisulthaan. Fa bi ayi alaa-i rabbikumaa tukassibaan. Yursalu 'alaikumaa shuwathum-min-naarin wa nuhaasun fala tantashiraan.

O company of Jinn and men, if ye have power to penetrate [all] regions of the heavens and the earth, then penetrate [them]! Ye will never penetrate them save with [Our] sanction. Which is it, of the favours of your Lord that ye deny? There will be sent, against you both, heat of fire and flash of brass, and ye will not escape.

Asking the Jinn to listen and get his attention, makes him more vulnerable and hurts him more. If talking to a Jinn and seeing that the discussion is useless, tell him, "Listen well!" He will say, "Yes?" And then one recites with full intensity.

Ask the Jinn if the recitation has burned him, and that he should recognize that the Qur'an is the Word of God. When he realizes this, he also realizes that Muhammad ﷺ is the Messenger of God.

The difference between da'wah for Jinn and da'wah for humans is that Jinn are much less complicated and more direct. When confronted with the truth, they usually surrender. An indisputable argument usually suffices to convince them, with the permission of Allāh.

However, if one fails to convince the Jinn that Islam is the truth, one should think again about what one might have done wrong and strengthen one's weak points. One should take care not to provoke the anger and the arrogance of the Jinn. Each time one should improve one's methods and never give up!

There are many reasons why a Jinn rejects or is reluctant to convert to Islam, even if he has already recognized the truth. If one recognize that something keeps him from doing so, one should ask him directly about it, or ask him if he wants to become a Muslim instead of commanding and exerting pressure on him. The gentle method is also more comfortable for the healer and the patient, and the Jinn could become a Muslim and useful to Islam.

The first reason why a Jinn rejects to convert to Islam is, he knows that he has to leave the body now. This he can not or does not want to because either magic locks him, or because he loves the patient, or he wants to revenge on him, or because the patient gives him shelter.

In these cases one must not try to convince him to go, but must separate faith and deeds: He can accept faith, even if he is not ready yet to practice immediately. One should preach him to love and to be grateful to God for what He has given him, and to take Him as his God and to accept His Prophet and His message.

The second reason why the Jinn is rejecting converting to Islam is because he has objections to it. It is in the responsibility of the Raqi to present Islam correctly. But beware! One should be sincere and do not try to deceive him! One should not say something if one is not sure.

The third reason is that the Jinn is not interested in religion or God. Then one should remember him of the grace of Allāh which He has shown us, and the advantages of religion in this world and in the world to come.

The fourth reason is that he still wants to revenge. One has to explain then that the patient has not intentionally injured him, and that he has already suffered enough and there is no reason to continue the revenge. And that forgiveness is an important virtue that leads one to paradise.

The fifth reason is that the Jinn does not want to leave the lover. One must ask him whether he himself would accept a forced marriage. Make it clear to him that Allāh does not accept a marriage between Jinn and human beings, and that he thereby oppresses and harms the man whom he pretends to love.

Of course one can not discuss with the Jinn forever. At some point he must be asked to leave the body, which of course he can not do if he is still locked with magic. One can ask him if he can remove the magic himself, which is unlikely, but one can try it.

If he can not, one should tell him to become a Muslim and ask Allāh to give him a way out and to heal the patient. Tell him that the effect of magic will be reduced during the following Qur'an recitation, and that he should then search for a gap and a way out. When one reads the Qur'an, the Jinn is burned and contracts and becomes extremely small to get burnt less. This makes it easier for him to leave the body, especially if we support it with hijamah. We inform him that we "help" him to leave the body by reading Qur'an and attacking the magic.

After that, the treatment methods should be resumed. If the Jinn then starts to scream, one gives him another opportunity, says to him the shahadah, and let him swear, not to enter into this or any other body in the future. Then he should leave and the patient regain consciousness.

The catching of Jinn

People who have ever been possessed by a Jinn have an "entrance" through which the Jinn has entered, and a "house" where the Jinn has been living in the body. With the Ruqya-bath it should be possible to close this entrance again. However, you can also use it to call Jinn by asking Allāh to let them come to you. And surprisingly, this seems to work very well, at least with Raqis of the caliber of Sheikh Abdur Raouf ben Halima. The Jinn so called can be brought to Islam and given the order to bring other Jinn to Islam or to bring them here. One can also interview them and get a lot of useful information. According to Sheikh Abdur Raouf, hundreds of thousands of Jinn have already been brought to Islam this way!

We have no experience with this method, but we want to list it here for the sake of completeness. The method is controversial because Ruqya is actually meant to protect oneself against Jinn and to drive them out or to kill them if necessary. Opponents of this method cite above all the following verse:

> In the day when He will gather them together [He will say]: O ye assembly of the Jinn! Many of humankind did ye seduce. And their adherents among humankind will say: Our Lord! We took advantage of one another, but now we have arrived at the appointed term which Thou appointedst for us. [Al-Anam 128]

They believe that this verse excludes that humans may have advantages of Jinn, and see the Prophet Sulaiman عليه السلام, who made great use of Jinn, as an exception. Sheikh Abdur Raouf, as an argument, cites a statement of

Sheikh al-Islam Ibn Taymiya, where he says in his book "Majmu al-Fatawa" Volume 11, p. 307:

"A human being who orders Jinn to do what Allah and His messenger have ordered, to worship Allah alone and obey his prophet, and also orders humans to do that, he is amongst the best allies of Allah the Almighty, and he becomes by this action a successor – caliph – and a representative of the messenger.

And the one who uses Jinn for authorized personal matters and orders them to do their duties and forbids them to commit what religion condemns and uses them in personal permitted matters, he is like the kings who did such things, and he who is capable of this is an ally of Allah the Almighty and like the prophet king compared to the prophet slave, like Sulayman and Yusuf compared to Ibrahim, Musa, Issa and Muhammad, may Allah bless them all.

And whoever uses Jinn for what Allah and his messenger have forbidden, either association (shirk), or to kill an innocent person, or harming people such as making them ill, or forget their science or commit a sin, this one has used their help for sin and harm, and if he uses them for acts considered as apostasy, he is an apostate.

And if his knowledge of Islamic rules is not complete and he uses their help for what he thinks to be miracles such as performing hajj, or flying, or they take him to Arafa and he doesn't perform the regular hajj, or they take him from city to city and so on, that one they drove him astray and tricked him".

Sheikh Abdur Raouf adds:

"The Prophet, blessing and peace be upon him, did not teach the roqya as he taught the worship and the religion; he left the field open and encouraged companions who practised it. He allowed people to treat as they want as long as they don't commit association - shirk."

I myself would like to avoid to judge and leave it to the reader to what extent he would like to practice this method. In any case, the dialogues that Sheikh Abdur Raouf has with the Jinn are very interesting and very entertaining too.

Control of violent Jinn

Violent Jinn are fortunately a small minority of Ruqya cases. Many of the Jinn will thrash around, scream, threaten, and try to scare; however, the number that are actually willing to carry out their threats are relatively small, and all praise is for Allāh سبحانه و تعال.

When one is dealing with truly violent Jinn, there are a few points to bear in mind:

➤ Your protection can only come from Allāh - place your trust completely in Him, and remember that Allāh is al-Qawiyy, al-Mateen - the Most Strong and the Most Powerful. If he protects you, there is nobody who can harm you, regardless of their strength.

➤ Make frequent requests, especially requests for overcoming an enemy:

$$اللَّهُمَّ إِنَّا نَجْعَلُكَ فِي نُحُورِهِمْ ،$$
$$وَنَعُوذُ بِكَ مِنْ شُرُورِهِمْ$$

Allāhumma innaa naj'aluka fie nuḥurihim, wa na'udhu bika min shururihim

O Allāh, we set you before them, and we seek refuge with you from their evil. [45]

➤ Do not try to overwhelm the Jinn by force. Many make this mistake, especially when they themselves are strong. They try to physically compete with the Jinn. But as explained in the chapter on Jinn, many Jinn are far superior to us physically, so that the patient in the truest sense of the word gets superhuman powers and

---

[45] Abu Dawood 1537; Al-Hakim 2629

often can hardly be restrained even with several people. One must therefore overwhelm the Jinn with the Qur'an. If one tries to fight them with force, they will usually win. If one tries to fight them with the Qur'an, they will lose with God's permission every time. Actually, the fact that the Jinn wants to attack one is a very good sign, because he is doing this because he already suffers and is close to losing.

➢ Consider not only your own safety, but also the patient's safety. Make sure that there is nothing in the room with which he could hurt himself. The majority of the violent Jinn will attack the patient before attacking the Raqi, so one should not leave dangerous objects in the room that could injure the patient or others.

➢ Don't allow the Jinn to intimidate you. The Jinn learn habits based on your reaction. If you let them hurt you and intimidate you, they will learn that they can get away with it, and do it all the time. If you put your foot down and teach the Jinn that misbehaviour will lead to severe punishment with Ruqya, then they will soon learn that shouting, screaming, and violence don't help.

➢ If you're struggling, keep some Ruqya water in a spray bottle and use it to subdue the Jinn. Not all Jinn are affected by it but for many of them it works.

➢ Try to get help from other people. Having more than one person makes you feel more confident, and helps you to deal with the issue in a way that is safer for you and for the patient.

➢ Be extremely cautious when physically restraining a patient, especially in countries which do not recognise Ruqya as a legitimate treatment, which are the majority. You will have trouble explaining that you have not beaten the patient, but the Jinn!

➢ Remember that your enemy doesn't overcome you because of his power, but because of your sin, so always take yourself to account, and repent. Success comes only from Allāh, and on the spiritual level taqwa (fearing God) has an immense effect which makes the strongest Jinn powerless.

The killing of the Jinn

There are several techniques to kill the Jinn. When he penetrates the body of a human being, human rules apply to him, which make him extremely vulnerable. One should be sure, however, that the Jinn is not a believer and is being blocked by magic and can not escape.

o   After having done the steps already mentioned, especially pointed out to the Jinn that he has to go or is being killed, one stretches the index finger of the right hand, speaks the confession of faith in Arabic (Aschado ala ilaha illAllāh wa aschado ana Muhammadar rasulAllāh) and recite Sura al-Anfal, verse 17 (or the verse of the throne, if one should not have memorized this verse):

$$\text{فَلَمْ تَقْتُلُوهُمْ وَلَـٰكِنَّ ٱللَّهَ قَتَلَهُمْ ۚ وَمَا رَمَيْتَ إِذْ رَمَيْتَ}$$
$$\text{وَلَـٰكِنَّ ٱللَّهَ رَمَىٰ ۚ وَلِيُبْلِيَ ٱلْمُؤْمِنِينَ مِنْهُ بَلَاءً حَسَنًا}$$
$$\text{إِنَّ ٱللَّهَ سَمِيعٌ عَلِيمٌ}$$

Falam taqtuluuhum wa laa kinnAllāha qatalahum. Wa maa ramaita isramaita wa laa kinnAllāha ramaa. Wa liyubliyal mu'miniena minhu bala-an hasanan. InnAllāha samie'un 'aliem.

Ye [Muslims] slew them not, but Allah slew them. And thou [Muhammad] threwest not when thou didst throw, but Allah threw, that He might test the believers by a fair test from Him. Lo! Allah is Hearer, Knower.

o   Pray to Allāh, e.g. as follows: "O Allāh, Creator of the heavens and the earth, who has power over all things, let this finger become a poisoned knife, extremely hot and sharp, which kills the Jinn in this body, O Lord!"

Then put the finger (or the knife in the subtle world) on the patient's neck. At this point, of course, the patient himself should no longer be conscious, or only half-conscious. The Jinn should feel the knife and react accordingly. Run your finger over the throat, as if you cut the patient's throat, from left to right and almost to the back. Normally the Jinn (the patient) will scream and make huge eyes. Repeat this if necessary. If one is successful, the patient's body will suddenly slacken, and shortly thereafter he will be conscious again. The Jinn, who had taken over the consciousness, is dead. A quite shocking spectacle for people who have never seen this before I may add.

o One can also use the above technique to cut off body parts of the Jinn. Instead of a knife, a saber is asked for, with the intention, e.g. to cut the legs of the Jinn to torment him. This gives the Jinn a last chance to regret and accept Islam. If he approves, one recites al-Fatihah in one's hand and wipes over the relevant spot with the intention of rejoining the body parts. After that, the confession of faith is recited to him, and, if he has repeated it twice, he has to swear to leave the body forever and also not to enter any other human body. If the Jinn was sincere, he will go out now and the patient will become consciousness. If the Jinn has lied, then he gets killed with the previous method.

o One recites al-Fatihah, the three Qul (al-Ikhlas, al-Falaq and An-Nas) and the verse of the throne and blows into one's hand, and repeats this procedure three to seven times. One touches the affected or painful spot while reciting the verse of the throne. Then one blows on the spot with the intention to burn the Jinn. This should be repeated three to seven times until the pain is gone.

- One can kill the Jinn in the dream as described in the chapter "Different treatment techniques".

- More techniques are also covered in the chapter "Treatment of Sihr". In fact, there are many techniques. Almost every Raqi has chosen the techniques which works best for him or developed his own over time. And normally one will see that the more faith a Raqi has, the less he needs, as the example of Imam Ahmad shows, who only had to send a sandal.

Treatment of Sihr

In the case of an enchantment / magic / sorcery, one must find the cause of the magic so that the disease can be cured.

> *Zayd ibn Arqam* رضي الله عنه *reported that a Jew named Labid Ibn Asam enchanted the Prophet* ﷺ. *When the Prophet* ﷺ *began to suffer under the effect, Jibril* عليه السلام *came to him, revealing to him the Mu'awidhatan (Sura Al-Falaq and An-Nas), saying, "Surely it was a Jew who uttered this spell upon you and the magical amulet is in a certain well." The Prophet* ﷺ *sent Ali ibn Abu Talib* رضي الله عنه *to bring the amulet. When he had come back with it, the Prophet* ﷺ *ordered him to untie the knots (of the amulet) one after the other, and to read a verse of the suras at every knot untied. After he had done this, the Prophet* ﷺ *appeared as if he had been freed from a bondage.* [46]

Perform the normal initial procedures as described in the chapter "The Healing". To find the Buhul, it is advisable to do it in the patient's house after it has been "cleaned" (from all pictures, etc.) and if possible sprayed with Ruqya water, because the Buhul could also be hidden in the house.

One way to find the Buhul is to ask the Jinn present in the patient. Of course it is obviuos that he is mostly lying, but one can try it, since Jinn are bad liars. With a little cross-examination one might find it.

---

[46] Ibn Humaid and Al-Bayhaqi

Otherwise, one recites Sura Al-Anam, verse 103, three or seven times:

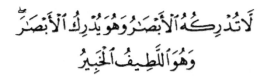

La tudrikuhul abshaaru wa huwa yudrikul abshaara wa huwal-lathieful chabier.

Vision comprehendeth Him not, but He comprehendeth [all] vision. He is the Subtile, the Aware.

Then pray to Allāh to show one the Buhul. Use names of Allāhs like "Ya Hadi" (the one giving guidance) - "Ya Wajid" (the all-finding and getting) - "Ya Latief" (the one who encompasses the most subtle in all dimensions) - "An-Nur" (the light) until the Buhul has found, whether by searching, inspiration or dream.

If the spell is tied to something outside the body, one destroys it as described in the Appendix (How to destroy a Buhul?).

If it is in the body, one can use the following method:

As usual, perform the initial procedures as described in the chapter "The Healing". One recites Sura Yasin, verse 9, with the intention of imprisoning the Jinn. Then blow on the index finger and the middle finger, and describe with them a circle around the affected area (counter-clockwise), either at the spot where the Buhul is suspected, or where it aches, itches, or there is a numb feeling.

$$\text{وَجَعَلْنَا مِنْ بَيْنِ أَيْدِيهِمْ سَدًّا}$$

$$\text{وَمِنْ خَلْفِهِمْ سَدًّا فَأَغْشَيْنَاهُمْ فَهُمْ لَا يُبْصِرُونَ}$$

Wa ja'alnaa min baini aidiehim saddan wa min chalfihim saddan fa-aghshainaahum fahum la yubshiruun.

And We have set a bar before them and a bar behind them, and [thus] have covered them so that they see not.

Then one recites Al-Anfal 17 and Al-Mu'minun 115 near the fingertips of the right hand and blows on them.

Al-Anfal 17

$$\text{فَلَمْ تَقْتُلُوهُمْ وَلَٰكِنَّ اللَّهَ قَتَلَهُمْ وَمَا رَمَيْتَ إِذْ رَمَيْتَ}$$

$$\text{وَلَٰكِنَّ اللَّهَ رَمَىٰ وَلِيُبْلِيَ الْمُؤْمِنِينَ مِنْهُ بَلَاءً حَسَنًا}$$

$$\text{إِنَّ اللَّهَ سَمِيعٌ عَلِيمٌ}$$

Falam taqtuluuhum wa laa kinnAllāha qatalahum. Wa maa ramaita isramaita wa laa kinnAllāha ramaa. Wa liyublial mu'miniena minhu bala-an hasanan. InnAllāha samie'un 'aliem.

Ye [Muslims] slew them not, but Allah slew them. And thou [Muhammad] threwest not when thou didst throw, but Allah threw, that He might test the believers by a fair test from Him. Lo! Allah is Hearer, Knower.

Al-Mu'minun 115

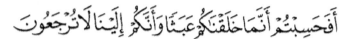

$$\text{أَفَحَسِبْتُمْ أَنَّمَا خَلَقْنَاكُمْ عَبَثًا وَأَنَّكُمْ إِلَيْنَا لَا تُرْجَعُونَ}$$

Afahasibtum annamaa chalaqnaakum 'abatsan wa annakum ilaina laturja'uun.

Deemed ye then that We had created you for naught, and that ye would not be returned unto Us?

Grasp the affected area with your fingertips (of course, do not clench too tightly), and, imagine, you pull out the disease / Jinn / spell, while saying "Bismillahi Allāhu akbar".

If one should not find the Buhul, it already helps to understand where it is hidden, e.g. hidden in a well or thrown into the sea, and what kind of magic it is. The patient will then already feel relief. References to where the Buhul is located come from the patient himself, usually in a dream: if he dreams, for example, of much water, one knows that it is in a river or in the sea; if he dreams of being at high altitudes, e.g. in an airplane or on a mountain, one knows that it is hanging on a tree; he dreams of graves and the dead, it is hidden in a cemetery, and so on.

The kind of spell also manifests itself through the patient: as shown in the above hadith, the Prophet ﷺ felt like tied, because the magic were knots. For example, if the patient says, "I am moving always in a circle," one knows that it is hung to a tree; if he says "I feel like dead," it means that it is in a graveyard.

In any case, the Ruqya-bath against sihr should be carried out like already described, especially when pulling out the magic should not work. In addition, one should also do cupping where the problem is, in order to pull out the magic or to allow it an exit. Furthermore, the house should be sprinkled with Ruqya-water, as described in the chapter "Variant of the Ruqya bath and cleaning of the house of Jinn or Sihr" and follow the general protective measures.

Returning the spell

Sorcery one should first only try to treat. If, however, it turns out that after the treatment the sorcerer sends more and more Jinn, one can consider sending the spell back to him, which is allowed under the Shariah (Qisas), although patience may be better:

> *If ye punish, then punish with the like of that wherewith ye were afflicted. But if ye endure patiently, verily it is better for the patient. [An-Nahl 126]*

Fighting the sorcerer is much more effective than fighting every time the Jinn, which has been sent.

One should gather the whole family of the patient and his close friends to pray together, which is more effective. Each one performs the initial procedure for himself as described in the chapter "The Healing". One should pray together the upcoming Compulsory Prayer and then 2 x 2 Rakaat Nawafil. During the last prostration one asks Allāh to return the magic and illness to the sorcerer or envious person. One begins the supplication best with *"Ya Hayyu ya Qayyum birahmatika astaghith"* (O Living, O Eternal, by your mercy I beg for help).

After the final Salaam one recites the Suras al-Fatihah, al-Ikhlas, al-Falaq, an-Nas, and the verse of the throne (see Appendix), three or seven times. Then Sura an-Nahl 26:

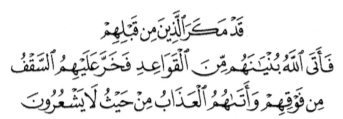

Qad makaral-lasina min qablihim, fa atAllāhu bunyaanahum-minal qawaa'idi facharra 'alaihimus-suqfu min fauqihim wa ataahumul 'asaabu min haitsu la yash'uruun.

Those before them plotted, so Allah struck at the foundations of their building, and then the roof fell down upon them from above them, and the doom came on them whence they knew not;

And Sura al-Fiel:

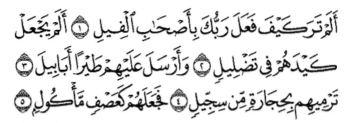

Alam tara kaifa fa'Ala rabbuka biashhaabil fiel. Alam yaj'al kaidahum fi tadhliel. Wa arsala 'alaihim thairann abaabiel. Tarmiehim bi hijaaratinm-min sijjiel. Faja'alahum ka'ashfinm-makuul.

Hast thou not seen how thy Lord dealt with the owners of the Elephant? Did He not bring their stratagem to naught, and send against them swarms of flying creatures, which pelted them with stones of baked clay, and made them like green crops devoured [by cattle]?

Recite these three, seven, or eleven times with all the ones assembled, with the intention of sending back the disease to the sorcerer. One should be sure that Allāh سبحانه و تعال accepts the petition of the oppressed, as the Prophet ﷺ said.

Psychotherapy

Mental problems often go hand in hand with problems caused by Jinn or magic, as they are mutually dependent. A mental problem gives the Jinn a "gap" through which they can penetrate, while the attack of Jinn can, on its part, trigger mental problems and usually also does. A mental problem can also create a mental field that blocks a Jinn, and without this problem being solved, the Jinn can not go out. Real healing must therefore take this aspect into account.

One can not expect any Raqi to be a psychotherapist, but there are a few simple measures that can create a valve for certain problems, which takes pressure from the patient and thus significantly increases the chance of achieving a complete healing.

Almost all patients will have experienced situations in their lives that have affected them emotionally very much, for example made them very sad, anxious or very angry. In similar situations, these emotions errupt again and can block the patient. Someone, who has been bitten by a dog, is usually afraid that this happens again and will mistrust dogs. Someone, who has once experienced a bad car accident, will get very nervous at higher speed. A woman, who has been raped, can be so traumatized that sexual intercourse becomes impossible for her.

Jinn and sorcerers can exploit such trauma to gain power over the person, for this mental world is the world of the Jinn. People, who are emotionally relaxed in stressful situations, are much less prone to Jinn attacks than nervous people and people with mental problems.

In order that the power of the Jinn over the person is reduced and future attacks become less likely, the psychological problem should be solved or at least psychological pressure should be released. A very simple method of doing this is the classic "couch method": one let's the patient talk about the event.

First, the patient is asked if he remembers an event in which he has suffered emotionally. Then one asks him to close his eyes and tell about it. When he reaches the painful part, he is asked to repeat the sentence describing his pain. And then he should tell the event again and describe it again, and then again.

The patient will go through various physical sensations such as headache, dizziness, fatigue or drowsiness. He will remember more details about the incident and recognize different things. And he will go through many emotions such as fear, sadness, anger or resentment until he can achieve positive emotions and maybe even laugh about it.

When there are no physical reactions, no new details come to light, and positive emotions occur, the mental pain has gone.

One asks him to look at the whole event again and see if there are still painful aspects, and if so, to talk about them again and tell them until a complete relief is achieved.

The patient is asked again to remember the incident until he is convinced that there is nothing more painful. Then one goes over to the next incident. One does not comment, one simply listens and asks, so that the patient remembers more details, always in the present, as if the incident were taking place here and now. One also asks, if one has the impression, he conceals something or does not express his pain properly.

Often, the patient himself will begin to talk about other events and one simply follows him. When the pain is expressed and thus the patient relieved, the knot is untied, and the patient can react normally and rationally again, and will not become victim of his emotions. And these emotions are often the reason why the therapy is blocked.

For example, if a woman became a victim of sexual violence, the Jinn, who has fallen in love with her or sexually abuses her, will hide in the part of her psyche that she avoids because of the pain she feels when she remembers.

The Raqi should explain to the patient why it is important to do such a therapy when one realizes that healing is blocked by mental problems. The psychological problem is many times the much greater ill, and the Jinn increases only the effect.

Final check and consulting

When the Ruqya is done, it still needs to be checked whether it was successful and no residue of the magic and no Jinn remain. We must look for signs that tell us.

There are Raqi who just need to look into one's eyes or grab one's hands to see if there is a Jinn or not. But for people who are not yet so professional, the following is recommended:

Put your hand on the patient's head and recite Sura Hud, verse 56.

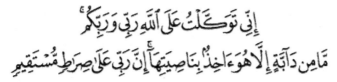

Inni tawakaltu 'alAllāhi rabbi wa rabbikum maa min daabbatin illa huwa achisun binaa shiyatihaa. Inna rabbi 'ala shiraathim-mustaqiem.

Lo! I have put my trust in Allah, my Lord and your Lord. Not an animal but He doth grasp it by the forelock! Lo! my Lord is on a straight path.

Or, recite al-Baqarah, verse 148, to call the Jinn again, if he is still in the body, or is still nearby, probably waiting to enter the body again.

وَلِكُلٍّ وِجْهَةٌ هُوَ مُوَلِّيهَا فَٱسْتَبِقُوا۟ ٱلْخَيْرَٰتِ أَيْنَ مَا تَكُونُوا۟ يَأْتِ بِكُمُ ٱللَّهُ جَمِيعًا إِنَّ ٱللَّهَ عَلَىٰ كُلِّ شَىْءٍ قَدِيرٌ

Wa likulli wijhatun huwa muwallihaa, fastabiquu al chairaat. Aina maa takunuu ya'tibikumullahu jami'aan. InnAllāha 'ala kulli shain qadir.

And each one hath a goal toward which he turneth; so vie with one another in good works. Wheresoever ye may be, Allah will bring you all together. Lo! Allah is Able to do all things.

If one has recited these verses several times and no reaction has taken place, the Ruqya was inshaAllāh successful.

However, with the treatment alone, it is usually not done yet. As already mentioned several times, the patient has to do the main effort himself. It is important to motivate him that from now on he carries out the protective measures consistently and, for the sake of precaution, does the 7-day program or the Ruqya-bath.

The more he follows the Sunnah of the Prophet ﷺ (see also the etiquettes of sleeping in the appendix), the more safe he will be in the future. Above all, he must understand that all healing and goodness comes from Allāh alone, and that he should fear Him and be grateful to Him.

If a patient refuses treatment

Some people have acquaintances or relatives who seem to have problems with Jinn or magic but do not want to be helped, perhaps because they do not believe in Ruqya or are already blocked by the Jinn. This raises the question of whether one may treat the person concerned with Ruqya without his knowledge or without his consent.

This is not recommended at all! First, it is illegal, and that could not only put the patient at risk, but the Raqi as well. In addition, it is very difficult from the perspective of Ruqya to treat a patient who does not cooperate. In such cases we would advise the following:

❖ It should be recognised that help comes only from Allāh. Therefore, one should turn to Him with much Du'a, night prayer and the like. When Allāh turns the heart of the patient to Islam and in search of the treatment he needs, there is no magic that can stop that.

❖ One should try to encourage and advise him. If he does not want to listen to one, then one should try if someone else can talk to him, whom he might want to listen to. The way people are convinced is obviously different for every person, but some people respond well to being challenged, like saying to them, "well, if there's nothing wrong with you, you won't mind having some Qur'an read over you." Some people respond very badly to that and they respond better to more positive messages and gentle encouragement. Sometimes it works not to tell people about Ruqya, but just to recommend that they go to see a certain Raqi and let the Raqi take the responsibility of convincing them of what needs to be done.

❖ Don't limit your encouragement to Ruqya alone. The patient most likely needs to do more to practise Islam - even more than they need Ruqya to be done. Ruqya can be of limited effectiveness with someone who isn't completely committed practising Islam anyway, as Satan has such a hold over them. Make sure that you begin by attaching their heart to Allah, convincing them to pray if they are not praying five times a day, and fulfilling the other basic Islamic obligations. Once the patient is doing those, you can slowly build them up to doing other good deeds, like reciting the Qur'an, and this will naturally bring them closer to Allah, and closer to seeking a cure from Him. Remember, that your actions and your belief come together, so if there are any issues in the patient's belief, such as seeking help from other than Allāh, traditional/cultural misconceptions, and so on, you need to clear those out first, before starting any Ruqya programme.

Travel to visit a Raqi

There is no doubt that the number of people seeking Ruqya has grown strongly. However, the desperate search for help, which is often associated with a lot of money and travels, is very problematic for the following reasons:

❖ From the perspective of trust in Allāh سبحانه و تعالى, it is problematic that a person travels hundreds of kilometers to search for Ruqya.

❖ From the point of view of money, it is wasteful.

❖ From the point of view of local patients, it violates their rights and burdens the Ruqya practitioners with a heavy burden.

❖ Most Ruqya cases are long-term and require a substantial investment in time that a traveling person simply can not afford.

❖ It leads to exaggeration, with hundreds of people who all want to the same Raqi, and say: "Travel to So-and-So, he has the best Ruqya!"

For these reasons, one should not consider treating a patient who is coming from outside the local area, unless the following conditions exist:

❖ The patient has already tried extensively to perform self-treatment and has strictly adhered to the instructions in this book.

❖ The patient strictly adheres to all important protective measures and Sunnahs, especially the mandatory prayers.

❖ The patient is a truly serious case, and is either exposed to considerable risk to his religion, or suffers a significant loss of quality in life.

❖ The patient has no other family members, friends or Raqi nearby that could help him.

Ruqya online

An alternative for the one who can not find a Raqi nearby is Ruqya online, e.g. via Skype or Viber. Of course, Ruqya is not so effective via Skype, but it can bring results. One will find websites on the Internet, which offer this even for free, or at least the first hour. One can try it, one has nothing to lose. In addition, there are of course many audios that one can listen to.

Websites which offer only the treatment, and charge around 50,- Euros per hour, but neither provide information and material for self-treatment, nor free treatment for people with little money, one should meet with skepticism. One should keep in mind that the treatment of a patient takes about 5-10 hours on average, often even more. If one meets the wrong person, it does not only cause damage to one's savings, but also to faith and trust in Ruqya!

Appendix

Ruqya-Suras and Verses

The following suras and verses are used in the treatments of this book. It is advisable to memorize them, but not to rely on transliteration, but rather with audio or, better, with a teacher. The transliteration has nevertheless been added to make instant Ruqya possible, even if one can not read Arabic or has not memorized the verses yet.

As said, Satan should not let convince oneself, the recitation would have no effect because the pronunciation is not yet one hundred per cent!

Al-Fatitah – The Opening

Bismillah-hir-rahman nir rahiem. Al-hamdulillah-hir-rabbil a'lameen, ar-rahman nir-raheem, maliki yaumid-deen. Iyyaka na' budu' wa iyyaka nasta'in. Ihdinas-sirathal mustaqeem, sirathal-lasina an amta alaihim, ghairil maghduubi alaihim wa lad-dhaalleen.

In the name of Allah, the Beneficent, the Merciful. Praise be to Allah, Lord of the Worlds, The Beneficent, the Merciful, Master of the Day of Judgment, Thee [alone] we worship; Thee [alone] we ask for help. Show us the straight path, the path of those whom Thou hast favoured; Not the [path] of those who earn Thine anger nor of those who go astray.

Al-Baqarah – The Cow 1-5

الٓمٓ ۝ ذَٰلِكَ ٱلْكِتَٰبُ لَا رَيْبَ ۛ فِيهِ ۛ هُدًى لِّلْمُتَّقِينَ ۝ ٱلَّذِينَ يُؤْمِنُونَ بِٱلْغَيْبِ وَيُقِيمُونَ ٱلصَّلَوٰةَ وَمِمَّا رَزَقْنَٰهُمْ يُنفِقُونَ ۝ وَٱلَّذِينَ يُؤْمِنُونَ بِمَآ أُنزِلَ إِلَيْكَ وَمَآ أُنزِلَ مِن قَبْلِكَ وَبِٱلْءَاخِرَةِ هُمْ يُوقِنُونَ ۝ أُو۟لَٰٓئِكَ عَلَىٰ هُدًى مِّن رَّبِّهِمْ ۖ وَأُو۟لَٰٓئِكَ هُمُ ٱلْمُفْلِحُونَ ۝

Alif lam miem. Salikal kitabu la ghaiba fiehi hudal-lil muttaqien. Allasina yu'minuuna bil ghaibi wa yuqiemuunash-sholata wa mimma rasaqnaahum yunfiquun. Wallasina yu'minuuna bimaa unsila ilaika wa maa unsila min qablika wa bil achirati hum yuuqinuun. Ulaaika 'ala hudam-mir-rabbihim, wa ulaaika humul muflihuun.

Alif. Lam. Mim. This is the Scripture whereof there is no doubt, a guidance unto those who ward off [evil]. Who believe in the Unseen, and establish worship, and spend of that We have bestowed upon them. And who believe in that which is revealed unto thee [Muhammad] and that which was revealed before thee, and are certain of the Hereafter. These depend on guidance from their Lord. These are the successful.

Al-Baqarah 148

وَلِكُلٍّ وِجْهَةٌ هُوَ مُوَلِّيهَا ۖ فَٱسْتَبِقُوا۟ ٱلْخَيْرَٰتِ ۚ أَيْنَ مَا تَكُونُوا۟ يَأْتِ بِكُمُ ٱللَّهُ جَمِيعًا ۚ إِنَّ ٱللَّهَ عَلَىٰ كُلِّ شَىْءٍ قَدِيرٌ

Wa likulli wijhatun huwa muwalliehaa, fastabiquu al chairaat. Aina maa takunuu ya'tibikumullahu jamie'aan. InnAllāha 'ala kulli schain qadier.

And each one hath a goal toward which he turneth; so vie with one another in good works. Wheresoever ye may be, Allah will bring you all together. Lo! Allah is Able to do all things.

Al-Baqarah 102

وَٱتَّبَعُواْ مَا تَتْلُواْ ٱلشَّيَٰطِينُ عَلَىٰ مُلْكِ سُلَيْمَٰنَ وَمَا كَفَرَ

سُلَيْمَٰنُ وَلَٰكِنَّ ٱلشَّيَٰطِينَ كَفَرُواْ يُعَلِّمُونَ ٱلنَّاسَ

ٱلسِّحْرَ وَمَآ أُنزِلَ عَلَى ٱلْمَلَكَيْنِ بِبَابِلَ هَٰرُوتَ وَمَٰرُوتَ

وَمَا يُعَلِّمَانِ مِنْ أَحَدٍ حَتَّىٰ يَقُولَآ إِنَّمَا نَحْنُ فِتْنَةٌ فَلَا

تَكْفُرْ فَيَتَعَلَّمُونَ مِنْهُمَا مَا يُفَرِّقُونَ بِهِۦ بَيْنَ ٱلْمَرْءِ

وَزَوْجِهِۦ وَمَا هُم بِضَآرِّينَ بِهِۦ مِنْ أَحَدٍ إِلَّا بِإِذْنِ ٱللَّهِ

وَيَتَعَلَّمُونَ مَا يَضُرُّهُمْ وَلَا يَنفَعُهُمْ وَلَقَدْ عَلِمُواْ لَمَنِ

ٱشْتَرَىٰهُ مَا لَهُۥ فِى ٱلْأَخِرَةِ مِنْ خَلَٰقٍ وَلَبِئْسَ مَا شَرَوْاْ بِهِۦٓ

أَنفُسَهُمْ لَوْ كَانُواْ يَعْلَمُونَ ۝

Wattaba'uu maa tatlusch-schayaathienu 'ala mulki sulaimaan, wa maa kafara sulaimaanu wa laakinnasch-schayaathiena kafaruu yu'allimuunan-naasas-sihra wa maa unsila 'alal malakaini bibaabila haaruuta wa maaruut, wa maa yu'allimaani min ahadin hatta yaqula innimaa nahnu fitnatun fala takfur, fayat'allamuuna minhumaa maa yufarriquunabihi bainal mari wa saujihi, wa maa hum bidhaar-rienabihi min ahadin illa bi isnillah, wa yata'allamuuna maa ya dhurruhum wa la yanfu'uhum, wa laqad 'alimuulamanisch taraahu maa lahu, fil achirati min chalaaq, wa la bi'sa maa scharaubihi anfusahum, lau kaanuu ya'lahuun.

And follow that which the devils falsely related against the kingdom of Solomon. Solomon disbelieved not; but the devils disbelieved, teaching mankind magic and that which was revealed to the two angels in Babel, Harut and Marut. Nor did they [the two angels] teach it to anyone till they had said: We are only a temptation, therefore disbelieve not [in the guidance of Allah]. And from these two [angles] people learn that by which they cause division between man and wife; but they injure thereby no-one save by Allah's leave. And they learn that which harmeth them and profiteth them not. And surely they do know that he who trafficketh therein will have no [happy] portion in the Hereafter; and surely evil is the price for which they sell their souls, if they but knew.

Al-Baqarah 255 – Ayat-ul-kursi

اللَّهُ لَا إِلَٰهَ إِلَّا هُوَ
الْحَىُّ الْقَيُّومُ لَا تَأْخُذُهُ سِنَةٌ وَلَا نَوْمٌ لَّهُ مَا فِى السَّمَٰوَٰتِ
وَمَا فِى الْأَرْضِ مَن ذَا الَّذِى يَشْفَعُ عِندَهُ إِلَّا بِإِذْنِهِ يَعْلَمُ
مَا بَيْنَ أَيْدِيهِمْ وَمَا خَلْفَهُمْ وَلَا يُحِيطُونَ بِشَىْءٍ مِّنْ عِلْمِهِ إِلَّا
بِمَا شَاءَ وَسِعَ كُرْسِيُّهُ السَّمَٰوَٰتِ وَالْأَرْضَ وَلَا يَئُودُهُ حِفْظُهُمَا
وَهُوَ الْعَلِىُّ الْعَظِيمُ ﴿٢٥٥﴾

Allāhu – la ilaaha illa huwal hayyul qayyuum, la ta'chusuhu sinatuw-wa la naum, lahu maa fis-samawaati wa maa fil ardh, man salasi yaschfa'u 'indahu illa bi isni, ya'lamu maa baina aidihim wa maa chalfahum, wa la yuhiethuuna bi shaim-min 'ilmihi illa bimaa shaa-a, wa si'a kursiyuhus-samawaati wal ardh, wa la ya uduhu hifsahuma, wa huwal 'aliyul 'athiem.

Allah! There is no god but He,- the Living, the Self-subsisting, Eternal. No slumber can seize Him nor sleep. His are all things in the heavens and on earth. Who is there can intercede in His presence except as He permitteth? He knoweth what [appeareth to His creatures as] before or after or behind them. Nor shall they compass aught of His knowledge except as He willeth. His Throne doth extend over the heavens and the earth, and He feeleth no fatigue in guarding and preserving them for He is the Most High, the Supreme [in glory].

Al-Baqarah 256

$$\text{لَآ إِكْرَاهَ فِى ٱلدِّينِ قَد تَّبَيَّنَ ٱلرُّشْدُ مِنَ}$$

$$\text{ٱلْغَيِّ فَمَن يَكْفُرْ بِٱلطَّٰغُوتِ وَيُؤْمِنۢ بِٱللَّهِ فَقَدِ ٱسْتَمْسَكَ}$$

$$\text{بِٱلْعُرْوَةِ ٱلْوُثْقَىٰ لَا ٱنفِصَامَ لَهَا وَٱللَّهُ سَمِيعٌ عَلِيمٌ ۝}$$

Laa ikraha fid-dien, qad-tabaiyanar-ruschdu minal ghaiy, faman yakfur bithooghuuti wa yu'mim billahi faqadis-tamsaka bil'urwatil-wusqaa lanfishoomalaha, wAllāhu sami'un 'aliem.

There is no compulsion in religion. The right direction is henceforth distinct from error. And he who rejecteth false deities and believeth in Allah hath grasped a firm handhold which will never break. Allah is Hearer, Knower.

Al-Baqarah 257

$$\text{ٱللَّهُ وَلِىُّ ٱلَّذِينَ ءَامَنُوا۟ يُخْرِجُهُم مِّنَ ٱلظُّلُمَٰتِ إِلَى ٱلنُّورِ}$$

$$\text{وَٱلَّذِينَ كَفَرُوٓا۟ أَوْلِيَآؤُهُمُ ٱلطَّٰغُوتُ يُخْرِجُونَهُم مِّنَ}$$

$$\text{ٱلنُّورِ إِلَى ٱلظُّلُمَٰتِ أُو۟لَٰٓئِكَ أَصْحَٰبُ ٱلنَّارِ هُمْ فِيهَا}$$

$$\text{خَٰلِدُونَ ۝}$$

Allāhu waliyyul-lasina amanu yuchrijuhum-minath-thulumaati ilan-nur, wallasina kafaruu auliyaa wuhumuth-thaaghuutu yuchriju nahum-minan-nuri ilath-thulumaat, uulaaika ash-haabun-nar, hum fieha chaliduun.

Allah is the Protecting Guardian of those who believe. He bringeth them out of darkness into light. As for those who disbelieve, their patrons are false deities. They bring them out of light into darkness. Such are rightful owners of the Fire. They will abide therein.

Al-Baqarah 284

$$\text{لِلَّهِ مَا فِى السَّمَوَاتِ}$$

$$\text{وَمَا فِى الْأَرْضِ وَإِن تُبْدُوا مَا فِى أَنفُسِكُمْ أَوْ تُخْفُوهُ}$$

$$\text{يُحَاسِبْكُم بِهِ اللَّهُ فَيَغْفِرُ لِمَن يَشَاءُ وَيُعَذِّبُ مَن يَشَاءُ}$$

$$\text{وَاللَّهُ عَلَى كُلِّ شَىْءٍ قَدِيرٌ ﴿٢٨٤﴾}$$

Lillahi maa fis-samawaati wa maa fil ardh, wa intubduumaa fie anfusikum autuchfuuhu yuhaasibkum bihilla, fayaghfiru limaiyaschaa-u wa yu'asibu maiyaschaa, wAllāhu ala kulli schain qadier.

Unto Allah [belongeth] whatsoever is in the heavens and whatsoever is in the earth; and whether ye make known what is in your minds or hide it, Allah will bring you to account for it. He will forgive whom He will and He will punish whom He will. Allah is Able to do all things.

Al-Baqarah 285

$$\text{ءَامَنَ الرَّسُولُ بِمَا أُنزِلَ إِلَيْهِ}$$

$$\text{مِن رَّبِّهِ وَالْمُؤْمِنُونَ كُلٌّ ءَامَنَ بِاللَّهِ وَمَلَائِكَتِهِ}$$

$$\text{وَكُتُبِهِ وَرُسُلِهِ لَا نُفَرِّقُ بَيْنَ أَحَدٍ مِّن رُّسُلِهِ وَقَالُوا}$$

$$\text{سَمِعْنَا وَأَطَعْنَا غُفْرَانَكَ رَبَّنَا وَإِلَيْكَ الْمَصِيرُ ﴿٢٨٥﴾}$$

Amanar-rasuulu bimaa unsila ilaihi mir-rabbihi wal mu'minuun, kullun amana billahi wa malaaikatihi wa kutubihi wa rasulihi, la nufar-riqu baina ahadim-mirrusulihi, wa qaalu sami'na wa atho'naa ghufraanaka wa ilaikal mashier.

The messenger believeth in that which hath been revealed unto him from his Lord and [so do] believers. Each one believeth in Allah and His angels and His scriptures and His messengers - We make no distinction

between any of His messengers - and they say: We hear, and we obey.
[Grant us] Thy forgiveness, our Lord. Unto Thee is the journeying.

Al-Baqarah 286

لَا يُكَلِّفُ
ٱللَّهُ نَفْسًا إِلَّا وُسْعَهَا لَهَا مَا كَسَبَتْ وَعَلَيْهَا مَا ٱكْتَسَبَتْ
رَبَّنَا لَا تُؤَاخِذْنَا إِن نَّسِينَا أَوْ أَخْطَأْنَا رَبَّنَا وَلَا تَحْمِلْ
عَلَيْنَا إِصْرًا كَمَا حَمَلْتَهُ عَلَى ٱلَّذِينَ مِن قَبْلِنَا رَبَّنَا
وَلَا تُحَمِّلْنَا مَا لَا طَاقَةَ لَنَا بِهِ وَٱعْفُ عَنَّا وَٱغْفِرْ لَنَا
وَٱرْحَمْنَا أَنتَ مَوْلَىٰنَا فَٱنصُرْنَا عَلَى ٱلْقَوْمِ ٱلْكَٰفِرِينَ ﴿٢٨٦﴾

La yukallifullahu nafsan illa wus'aha, laha maa kasabat wa 'alaihaa
maktasabat, rabbana la tuaachisnaa in-nasiena au achtho'na, rabbana
wa la tahmil 'alaina ishran kamaa hamaltahu 'alallasina min qoblina,
rabbana wa la tuhammilna maa la thaa qatalanabihi, wa'fu'anna,
waghfirlana, warhamna, anta maulaana fanshurnaa 'alal qaumil
kaafirien.

Allah tasketh not a soul beyond its scope. For it [is only] that which it
hath earned, and against it [only] that which it hath deserved. Our Lord!
Condemn us not if we forget, or miss the mark! Our Lord! Lay not on us
such a burden as thou didst lay on those before us! Our Lord! Impose
not on us that which we have not the strength to bear! Pardon us,
absolve us and have mercy on us, Thou, our Protector, and give us
victory over the disbelieving folk.

Al-Anam – Cattle 103

لَّا تُدْرِكُهُ ٱلْأَبْصَٰرُ وَهُوَ يُدْرِكُ ٱلْأَبْصَٰرَ
وَهُوَ ٱللَّطِيفُ ٱلْخَبِيرُ

La tudrikuhul abshaaru wa huwa yudrikul abshaara wa huwal-lathieful chabier.

Vision comprehendeth Him not, but He comprehendeth [all] vision. He is the Subtile, the Aware.

Al-Araf – The Heights 117-122

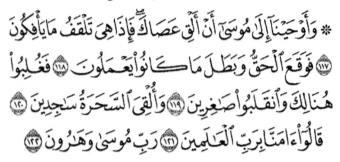

Wa au hainaa ila muusa an alqi 'ashoka fa isa hiya talqafu maa ya'fikum. Fawaqa'alhaqqu wa bathola maa kaanuu ya'maluun. Faghulibuu hunaalika wanqalabuu shoghirien. Walqiyas-saharatu saajidien. Qaaluu amanna birabbil'aalamien. Rabbi muusa wa haaruun.

And We inspired Moses [saying]: Throw thy staff! And lo! it swallowed up their lying show. Thus was the Truth vindicated and that which they were doing was made vain. Thus were they there defeated and brought low. And the wizards fell down prostrate, Crying: We believe in the Lord of the Worlds, The Lord of Moses and Aaron.

Al-Anfal – Spoils of war 17

فَلَمْ تَقْتُلُوهُمْ وَلَٰكِنَّ ٱللَّهَ قَتَلَهُمْ وَمَا رَمَيْتَ إِذْ رَمَيْتَ
وَلَٰكِنَّ ٱللَّهَ رَمَىٰ وَلِيُبْلِيَ ٱلْمُؤْمِنِينَ مِنْهُ بَلَآءً حَسَنًا
إِنَّ ٱللَّهَ سَمِيعٌ عَلِيمٌ

Falam taqtuluuhum wa laa kinnAllāha qatalahum. Wa maa ramaita isramaita wa laa kinnAllāha ramaa. Wa liyubliyal mu'miniena minhu bala-an hasanan. InnAllāha samie'un 'aliem.

Ye [Muslims] slew them not, but Allah slew them. And thou [Muhammad] threwest not when thou didst throw, but Allah threw, that He might test the believers by a fair test from Him. Lo! Allah is Hearer, Knower.

Yunus – Jonah 79-82

وَقَالَ فِرْعَوْنُ ٱئْتُونِي بِكُلِّ سَاحِرٍ عَلِيمٍ ۝ فَلَمَّا جَآءَ ٱلسَّحَرَةُ قَالَ لَهُم مُّوسَىٰٓ أَلْقُوا۟ مَآ أَنتُم مُّلْقُونَ ۝ فَلَمَّآ أَلْقَوْا۟ قَالَ مُوسَىٰ مَا جِئْتُم بِهِ ٱلسِّحْرُ إِنَّ ٱللَّهَ سَيُبْطِلُهُۥٓ إِنَّ ٱللَّهَ لَا يُصْلِحُ عَمَلَ ٱلْمُفْسِدِينَ ۝ وَيُحِقُّ ٱللَّهُ ٱلْحَقَّ بِكَلِمَٰتِهِۦ وَلَوْ كَرِهَ ٱلْمُجْرِمُونَ ۝

Wa qaala fira'unu'tuni bikulli saahirin 'aliem. Falamma dschaa as-saharatu qaala lahum muusa alquu maa antum mulquun. Falamma alqau qaala muusa maa dschi'tum bihis-sihru, innAllāha sayubthiluhu, innAllāha la yushlihu 'amalal mufsiduun. Wa yuhiqqullahul haqqa bikalimaatihi, wa lau karihal mudschrimuun.

And Pharaoh said: Bring every cunning wizard unto me. And when the wizards came, Moses said unto them: Cast your cast! And when they had cast, Moses said: That which ye have brought is magic. Lo! Allah will make it vain. Lo! Allah upholdeth not the work of mischief-makers. And Allah will vindicate the Truth by His words, however much the guilty be averse.

Hud 56

إِنِّي تَوَكَّلْتُ عَلَى ٱللَّهِ رَبِّي وَرَبِّكُم مَّا مِن دَآبَّةٍ إِلَّا هُوَ ءَاخِذٌۢ بِنَاصِيَتِهَآ إِنَّ رَبِّي عَلَىٰ صِرَٰطٍ مُّسْتَقِيمٍ

Inni tawakaltu 'alAllāhi rabbi wa rabbikum maa min daabbatin illa huwa achisun binaa shiyatihaa. Inna rabbi 'ala shiraathim-mustaqiem.

Lo! I have put my trust in Allah, my Lord and your Lord. Not an animal but He doth grasp it by the forelock! Lo! my Lord is on a straight path.

An-Nahl – The bee 26

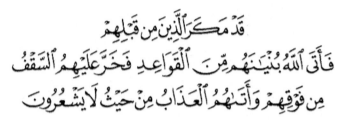

قَدْ مَكَرَ ٱلَّذِينَ مِن قَبْلِهِمْ فَأَتَى ٱللَّهُ بُنْيَنَهُم مِّنَ ٱلْقَوَاعِدِ فَخَرَّ عَلَيْهِمُ ٱلسَّقْفُ مِن فَوْقِهِمْ وَأَتَىٰهُمُ ٱلْعَذَابُ مِنْ حَيْثُ لَا يَشْعُرُونَ

Qad makaral-lasina min qablihim, fa atAllāhu bunyaanahum-minal qawaa'idi facharra 'alaihimus-suqfu min fauqihim wa ataahumul 'asaabu min haitsu la yasch'uruun.

Those before them plotted, so Allah struck at the foundations of their building, and then the roof fell down upon them from above them, and the doom came on them whence they knew not.

Taha 65-69

قَالُوا۟ يَٰمُوسَىٰٓ إِمَّآ أَن تُلْقِىَ وَإِمَّآ أَن نَّكُونَ أَوَّلَ مَنْ أَلْقَىٰ ۝ قَالَ بَلْ أَلْقُوا۟ فَإِذَا حِبَالُهُمْ وَعِصِيُّهُمْ يُخَيَّلُ إِلَيْهِ مِن سِحْرِهِمْ أَنَّهَا تَسْعَىٰ ۝ فَأَوْجَسَ فِى نَفْسِهِۦ خِيفَةً مُّوسَىٰ ۝ قُلْنَا لَا تَخَفْ إِنَّكَ أَنتَ ٱلْأَعْلَىٰ ۝ وَأَلْقِ مَا فِى يَمِينِكَ تَلْقَفْ مَا صَنَعُوٓا۟ إِنَّمَا صَنَعُوا۟ كَيْدُ سَٰحِرٍ وَلَا يُفْلِحُ ٱلسَّاحِرُ حَيْثُ أَتَىٰ ۝

Qaaluu yaa muusa imma an tulqiya wa imma an-nakuuna auwala man alqa. Qaala bal alquu, fa isa hibaaluhum wa 'ishiyuhum yuchaiyalu ilaihi min sihrihim annahaa tas'aa. Fa audschasa fie nafsihie chiefatam-muusa. Qulnaa la tachaf innaka antal 'ala. WA alqi maa fie yamienika talqaf maa shana'uu, innamaa shana'uu kaidu saahirin wa la yuflihus-saahiru haisu ataa.

They said: O Moses! Either throw first, or let us be the first to throw? He said: Nay, do ye throw! Then lo! their cords and their staves, by their magic, appeared to him as though they ran. And Moses conceived a fear in his mind. 68. We said: Fear not! Lo! thou art the higher. Throw that which is in thy right hand! It will eat up that which they have made. Lo! that which they have made is but a wizard's artifice, and a wizard shall not be successful to whatever point [of skill] he may attain.

Al-Mu'minoon – The believers 115

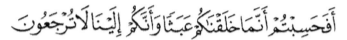

Afahasibtum annamaa chalaqnaakum 'abatsan wa annakum ilaina laturja'uun.

Deemed ye then that We had created you for naught, and that ye would not be returned unto Us?

Yasin 9

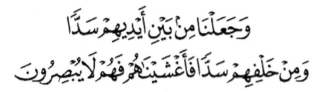

Wa ja'alnaa min baini aidiehim saddan wa min chalfihim saddan fa-aghschainaahum fahum la yubshiruun.

And We have set a bar before them and a bar behind them, and [thus] have covered them so that they see not.

Ar-Rahman – The Beneficent 33-35

يَٰمَعْشَرَ ٱلْجِنِّ وَٱلْإِنسِ إِنِ ٱسْتَطَعْتُمْ
أَن تَنفُذُوا۟ مِنْ أَقْطَارِ ٱلسَّمَٰوَٰتِ وَٱلْأَرْضِ فَٱنفُذُوا۟ لَا تَنفُذُونَ
إِلَّا بِسُلْطَٰنٍ ۝ فَبِأَىِّ ءَالَآءِ رَبِّكُمَا تُكَذِّبَانِ ۝ يُرْسَلُ عَلَيْكُمَا
شُوَاظٌ مِّن نَّارٍ وَنُحَاسٌ فَلَا تَنتَصِرَانِ ۝

Yaa m'aschral Jinni wal insi inistata'tum an tanfusuu min aqthaaris-
samawaati wal ardhi fanfusuu. La tanfusuuna illa bisulthaan. Fa bi ayi
alaa-i rabbikumaa tukassibaan. Yursalu 'alaikumaa schuwathum-min-
naarin wa nuhaasun fala tantashiraan.

O company of Jinn and men, if ye have power to penetrate [all] regions
of the heavens and the earth, then penetrate [them]! Ye will never
penetrate them save with [Our] sanction. Which is it, of the favours of
your Lord that ye deny? There will be sent, against you both, heat of fire
and flash of brass, and ye will not escape.

Al-Fiel – The Elephant

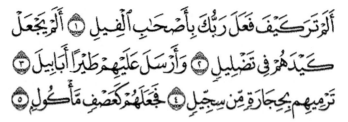

Alam tara kaifa fa'Ala rabbuka biashhaabil fiel. Alam yaj'al kaidahum fi
tadhliel. Wa arsala 'alaihim thairann abaabiel. Tarmiehim bi hijaaratinm-
min sijjiel. Faja'alahum ka'ashfinm-makuul.

Hast thou not seen how thy Lord dealt with the owners of the Elephant?
Did He not bring their stratagem to naught, And send against them
swarms of flying creatures, Which pelted them with stones of baked
clay, And made them like green crops devoured [by cattle]?

Al-Ikhlas – Purity of Faith

Qul huwal-lahu ahad, al-lahus-samad, lam yalid wa lamyuulad, wa lam yakul-lahu kufu-wan ahad.

Say: He is Allah, the One and Only; Allah, the Eternal, Absolute; He begetteth not, nor is He begotten; and there is none like unto Him.

Al-Falaq – The dawn

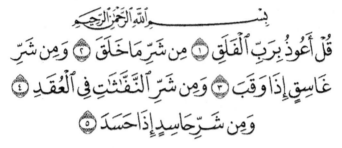

Qul a'usu birabbil falaq, min scharri maa chalaq, wa min scharri ghaasiqin isa waqab, wa min scharrin-naffaasaati fil 'uqad. Wa min sharri hasideen isa hasad.

Say: I seek refuge with the Lord of the Dawn From the mischief of created things; from the mischief of Darkness as it overspreads; from the mischief of those who practise secret arts; and from the mischief of the envious one as he practises envy.

An-Naas – Mankind

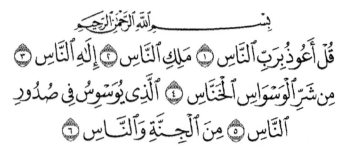

Qul 'ausubirabbin-naas, malikin-naas, ilaahin-naas, min sharril waswaasil channaas, allasi yuwaswisu fie shuduurin-naas, minal Jinnati wan-naas.

Say: I seek refuge with the Lord and Cherisher of Mankind, The King of Mankind, The god [or judge] of Mankind, from the mischief of the Whisperer [of Evil], who withdraws [after his whisper], [The same] who whispers into the hearts of Mankind, Among Jinn and among men.

Other verses, which are often used during Ruqya:

- ❖ Al-Baqarah 6-10; 163-164
- ❖ Ali Imran 18-19
- ❖ Al-Araf 54-56
- ❖ Al-Mu'minoon 116-118
- ❖ As-Saffat 1-10
- ❖ Al-Ahqaf 29-32
- ❖ Al-Hashr 21-24
- ❖ Al-Jin 1-9
- ❖ Al-Kafiroon

Etiquettes of prayer

Prayer (Du'a) is one of the most important things in Ruqya (and, of course, in life in general) and one of the most important factors whether Ruqya works because healing comes from Allāh alone. When our prayer is accepted, healing is almost certain. That is why it is important to know how our prayer is better accepted by Allāh.

Concerning the Shalat, it is obvious that one should perform it at the beginning of its time, perform it according to the Prophet's ﷺ Sunnah, and be humble and concentrated. During Du'a, the voluntary supplication, the following points should be observed:

1. One must realize that only Allāh responds to prayer and no one else has any power.

2. It follows that one should only ask Allāh for anything.

3. *Tawassul* is an important aspect of prayer. Linguistically it means "coming closer to a goal". In Islam, it means using methods that help the prayer being accepted.

   a. Tawassul with Allāh's names and attributes. The Koran teaches us that Allāh loves prayers, in which His glorious names and attributes are mentioned. Our prayer gets more depth. We should name the particular attribute, which corresponds to our request, e.g. ar-Razaq when we ask for livelihood.

   b. Tawassul by listing the good things given to us by God. This will strengthen our love for Allāh and the bond to Him.

    c. The mentioning of one's own condition helps one to recognize one's own weakness and being in need. But beware of self-pity!

4. One should explicitly name what one wants and what one would do if one would get it.

5. Impatience can be a reason why our prayer is not accepted. (*And man supplicates for evil as he supplicates for good, and man is ever hasty.* [Al-Isra' 11])

6. We should, of course, only ask for pure and good things, and let not ourselves be dominated by feelings of hatred and revenge.

7. Very important is the right intention as with everything we do. We should always check it.

8. We should make the prayer with an attentive heart, and not just babble it down.

9. One should ensure that one's own livelihood is "halal", otherwise the prayer is not well received (if at all).

10. Prayer should include Salawat (Blessings on the Prophet).

11. The Du'a should not deter one from more important things, eg. the obligatory prayer.

12. One should praise Allāh before prayer. Whoever does not do this is called hasty.

13. One should raise one's hands with hands upwards.

14. One should pray in the direction of the Kiblat.

15. One should be in the state of ritual purity.

16. If one can, one should cry.

17. One should hope for the best from Allāh.

18. Pray with humility and *taqwa* (God-fearingness).

19. One should confess one's needs only to Allāh.

20. Pray softly and not with a loud voice.

21. Admit and repent your sins.

22. When one asks, one should be brave and show Allāh how necessary one needs an answer.

23. Repeat the prayer three times, which highlights the importance of the petition.

24. Prayer should be short, but much comprising, e.g. for the good in this world (and Allāh knows best what is good for us), and for the good in the hereafter (which only He knows).

25. One should pray for oneself first and then for others.

26. One should say "Ameen", which means "accept" (the prayer).

27. One should pray all the time, not just when one has problems again.

28. One should also pray for the little things in life. Allāh loves to be asked.

29. There are certain situations in which prayer is better accepted:

    a. When one is oppressed or one has suffered an injustice.

    b. When one is in distress.

    c. After a hard trial, where one remained patient.

    d. During travel.

e. When one fasts.

f. When one reads the Qur'an.

g. During Haj, Umrah or Jihad.

h. Prayer for someone in his absence.

i. If one always remembers Allāh.

j. If one is a righteous ruler.

30. There are certain times when prayer is better accepted:

a. In the last third of the night.

b. During *Azan* (prayer call).

c. Between *Azan* and *Iqamah*.

d. During the mandatory prayer.

e. During the prostration.

f. Before the *Salam* of the mandatory prayer.

g. After the obligatory prayer.

h. A certain time on Friday, so one should pray a lot on Friday.

i. Between the two *Khutbas* (sermons) of the Friday prayer.

j. When one has read the whole of the Qur'an.

k. After the ablution for prayer.

l. Before drinking Zam-Zam-water.

m. During Ramadhan.

n. In the "Night of power", most likely in the night of the 27th Ramadan.

o. When one visits the sick.

p. While it is raining (not during a storm or devastating rainfall).

q. The time before the Dhuhur prayer.

r. When a rooster crows.

The etiquettes of sleeping

The Sunnahs of the evening and night are very important as they provide protection at a time when the Satans are the most active, but at the same time our defense is weak. However, the Adhkaar listed here are very extensive (though not by far all of them have been cited), and the normal Muslim will surely be overwhelmed to practice it all. So everyone should choose for himself what he likes best and most importantly, what he can practice regularly! It is much better to do little, but regularly, as much, but only occasionally as the Prophet ﷺ told us:

> 'Aishah رضي الله عنه reported that the Prophet ﷺ said: "The deeds which Allāh loves most are those that are done regularly, even if they are few."[47]

There are, however, Adhkaar which are more important, and give more protection and more reward than others.

It is also good to change the routine sometimes, so that one is more attentive. Probably the Prophet ﷺ and his companions did so, because it is hardly conceivable that they recited the entire Adhkaar every evening completely.

The night is for sleeping and for worship. This order arranged Allāh Himself. Whoever makes the night a day is acting against this order and has to expect negative consequences.

> He it is Who hath appointed for you the night that ye should rest therein and the day giving sight. Lo! herein verily are portents for a folk that heed. [Yunus 67]

---

[47] Bukhari, Muslim

Sleep is one of the conditions in which we are most vulnerable. We should therefore prepare ourselves for it, not only because we protect ourselves, but also because we get great reward during sleep if we do it according the Sunnah, and in this way becomes worship at a time when the Evil is most active.

> Jabir رضي الله عنه reported that the Prophet ﷺ said, "When the darkness of night sets in, the devils spread about."[48]

> And Jabir also reported that the Prophet ﷺ said, "After the quietness (of night), lessen your ventures outdoors, for, indeed, Allah has creatures that He then lets loose."[49]

So we see that the night is a time when evil is more active, be it dangerous animals, Jinn, magic, and evil people. The Prophet ﷺ has given us instructions, so that we may be safer during this time.

The best protection against the evils of this world is God-remembrance (Dhikr), which in this context means to remember and praise Allāh.

> ... and hymn the praise of thy Lord before the rising and before the setting of the sun. And in the night-time hymn His praise, and after the [prescribed] prostrations. [Qaf 39-40]

> Al-Harith al-Ash'ari رضي الله عنه reported that the Prophet ﷺ said, "...And I command you to extoll Allah. The example of this is like that of a man who is being closely chased by enemies — until he reaches a secure fortress where he takes shelter

---

[48] Bukhari (3304, 5623), Muslim (2012, 2013), and others
[49] Abu Dawood and Bukhari

against them. Similarly, a person cannot protect himself from Satan except by extolling Allah"[50]

Jabir رضي الله عنه reported that the Prophet ﷺ said, "When a person invokes Allah upon entering his home and over his food, Satan tells his allies, "There is no lodging or food for you (in this house tonight)." But if that person enters his home without invoking Allah, Satan says to his allies, 'You have secured lodging.' And if he does not invoke Allah over his food, Satan says, 'You have secured both lodging and food.' "[51]

When the sun goes down, the children should be kept indoors to protect them from the evils of the night, especially between the evening and the night prayer, since the Satans are most active then.

*Jabir رضي الله عنه reported that the Prophet ﷺ said: When the night sets in, restrain your children (from playing) until the peak of dusk ends, because devils spread at that time. When an hour of the night has passed, you may release them." *[52]

The children may go out after the night prayer but if it becomes late at night and the streets get empty, nobody should stay outside without an important reason.

We should lock the doors and windows and pronounce the name of Allāh („Bismillah").

Jabir Bin 'Abdillah رضي الله عنه reported that the Prophet ﷺ said: „When the night sets in, close the doors and utter Allah's name over them. Indeed,

---

[50] Tirmithi, Ibn Hibban, and others
[51] Muslim (2018) and Abu Dawood
[52] Bukhari, Muslim and others

Satan would not open a closed door upon which Allah's Name was uttered."[53]

We should cover food and beverages during the night by pronouncing the name of Allāh.

Jabir Bin 'Abdillah رضي الله عنه reported that the Prophet ﷺ said: "When the night sets in, close large jars and tie the water skins, and pronounce Allah's name; and cover food vessels — even if only by placing a stick across their opening, and pronounce Allah's name. Indeed, the Devil would not open or uncover closed vessels."[54]

When we go to bed we should extinguish all fires and lamps.

'Abdullah Bin 'Umar رضي الله عنه and Abu Musa al-Ash'ari رضي الله عنه reported that the Prophet ﷺ said: „Do not leave the fire lighted in your homes when you go to sleep, because it is an enemy to you. So when you go to sleep, extinguish it."[55]

Important Adhkaar of the evening / night

Some Adhkaar listed below are already mentioned under protective measure. One finds the Suras and verses also at the beginning of the appendix.

'Abdullah Bin Khubayb رضي الله عنه reported that he went with other men on a dark and rainy night seeking the Prophet ﷺ to lead them in prayer. When they found him, the Prophet ﷺ said to Khubayb, "Say!" Not knowing what to say, Khubayb remained

---

[53] Bukhari (3304, 5623), Muslim (2112, 2013)
[54] Bukhari, Muslim
[55] Bukhari (6293, 6294), Muslim (2015, 2016)

silent. The Prophet ﷺ made the same demand two more times. On the third time, Khubayb said, "O Allah's Messenger, what should I say?" The Prophet ﷺ replied: "Say 'Qul huw-allahu ahad' (Sura al-Ikhlas) and the muawwithatan (Sura al-Falaq & Sura An-Nas) three times in the evening and in the morning. This would protect you from all (harmful) things."[56]

———

Abu Masud al-Ansari رضي الله عنه reported that the Prophet ﷺ said: „Whoever recites the two ayat at the end of surat ul-Baqarah (verses 285 & 286) at night, they suffice him (as protection for that night."[57]

———

Shaddad Bin Aws رضي الله عنه reported that the Prophet ﷺ teached his companions the following Adhkaar (Sayyidul Istighfar) and indicated that whoever recites it during the evening and dies during the night, will go to paradise[58]:

«اللَّهُمَّ أنتَ رَبِّي، لا إلَهَ إلا أنتَ، خَلَقْتَنِي وأنا عَبْدُكَ، وأنا عَلى عهْدِكَ ووَعْدِكَ ما اسْتَطَعْتُ، أَعوذُ بكَ مِنْ شَرِّ ما صَنَعْتُ، أبوءُ لكَ بِنِعْمَتِكَ عَلَيَّ، وأبوءُ بذَنْبِي، فاغْفِرْ لي، فإنَّهُ لا يَغْفِرُ الذُّنوبَ إلا أنتَ.»

---

[56] Abu Dawood, at-Tirmithi, and others
[57] Bukhari (5008, 5009) and Muslim (808)
[58] Bukhari (6306), an-Nasa'i, and others

Allāhumma anta Rabbi, la ilaha illa anta, khalaqtani, wa ana 'abduka, wa ana 'ala 'ahdika wa wa'dika mastata't, authubika min sharri ma sana't, abu'u laka bi ni'matika alayya, wa abu'u bisanbi, faghfirli, fa innahu la yaghfiruth thunuba illa ant.

O Allah, You are my Lord, and there is no (true) god but You. You created me, and I am Your servant, and I try to fulfill my covenant and promise to You as much as I am able. I seek Your protection from the evil of my doings. I admit Your favors upon me, and I confess my sins to You, so forgive me, because no one forgives sins but You.

———

'Abdullah Bin 'Amr and Abu Hurayrah رضي الله عنه *reported that the Prophet ﷺ said, promised for a person who says this extollment one hundred times in the evening:*

لَا إِلَهَ إِلَّا اللّٰهُ ، وَحْدَهُ لَا شَرِيكَ لَهُ ،
لَهُ الْمُلْكُ وَلَهُ الْحَمْدُ ، يُحْيِي وَيُمِيتُ ،
وَهُوَ عَلَى كُلِّ شَيْءٍ قَدِيرٌ

Laa ilaaha ill-Allāhu, waḥdahu laa sharika lahu, lahul-mulku wa lahul-ḥamdu, yuḥyi wa yumitu, wa huwa 'alaa kulli shay'in qadir.

There is no (true) god except Allah, alone and without any partners. To Him belongs the dominion, He deserves all praise. He gives life and death, and He is capable of everything.

This will count for him as freeing ten slaves; and one hundred good deeds will be recorded for him, one hundred sins will be removed from his record, and this will provide for him a shelter from Satan until the morning; and no one will come (on Judgment

Day) with a better deed except for a man who exceeded him (in saying it [59]

But for reciting the above mentioned Adhkaar just 10-times, Allah will record for him for every one extollment ten good deeds, will remove from his record ten sins, and will raise him ten ranks (in Jannah), and they will count for him as freeing ten slaves. Allah will also protect him from Satan, and they will shield him from the beginning until the end of the night.[60]

And for reciting the Adhkaar just once in the evening, it will count for him as freeing one slave from Ismail's offspring, ten good deeds will be recorded for him, ten sins will be removed from his record, he will be raised ten ranks (in paradise), and he will be protected from Satan until the morning.[61]

———

---

[59] Bukhari (6403), Muslim (2691), Nasa'i, Ahmad and others
[60] Ahmad, an-Nasa'i and at-Tabarani
[61] Abu Dawud, an-Nasa'i, and others

The Adhkaar mentioned above are inshaAllāh the most important ones. But for those who want to do more, here are listed a few more:

Ibn Mas'ud reported that the Prophet ﷺ used to say in the evening:

«أمْسَيْنا وأمْسى الْمُلْكُ لله، والْحَمْدُ لله. لآ إِلهَ إلاَّ اللهُ وَحْدَهُ لا شَرِيكَ لَهُ، لهُ الْمُلْكُ، وله الْحَمْدُ، وهُوَ على كُلِّ شَيْءٍ قديرٌ. رَبِّ أسألُكَ خَيْرَ ما فِي هَذِهِ اللّيْلَةِ، وخيرَ ما بَعْدَها، وأعوذُ بكَ مِنْ شَرِّ ما فِي هَذِهِ اللّيْلَةِ، وشرِّ ما بَعْدَها، رَبِّ أعوذُ بكَ مِنَ الكَسَلِ، وَسُوءِ الْكِبَرِ. رَبِّ أعوذُ بكَ مِنْ عذابٍ في النّارِ، وعذابٍ في الْقَبْرِ.»

Amsayna wa-amsal mulku lillah, wal-hamdu lillah. La ilaaha illAllāhu wahdahu la sharika lahu, lahul- mulku wa-lahul hamd, wa-huwa 'ala kulli shayin qadir. Rabbi asaluka khayra maa fie hathihil laylati wa- khayra maa badaha, wa-authu bika min sharri maa fie hathihil laylati wa-sharri maa badaha. Rabbi authu bika minal kasali wa-suuil kibar. Rabbi authu bika min 'athabin fin-nari wa-athabin fil-qabr.

We have reached the morning, and the dominion continues to belong to Allah — all praise be to Allah. There is no (true) god but Allah, alone without any partner. To Him belongs the dominion, He is worthy of all praise, and He is capable of everything. My Lord, I ask You for the goodness of this day and of what comes after it, and seek your protection from the evil of this day and of what comes after it. My Lord, I (also) seek your protection from laziness, from the evil of old age, from the punishment in the Fire, and from the punishment in the grave.[62]

———

———

[62] Muslim, Abu Dawood and others

Abu Hurayrah رضي الله عنه *reported that the Prophet* ﷺ *used to say in the evening and teached it to his companions:*

«اللَّهُمَّ بِكَ أَمْسَيْنا، وَبِكَ أَصْبَحْنا،
وَبِكَ نَحْيا وَبِكَ نَمُوتُ، وَإِلَيْكَ الْمَصِيرُ.»

Allāhumma bika amsayna, wa-bika asbahna, wa-bika nahya, wa-bika namut, wa-ilayk al-masir.

O Allah, by You (i.e., Your will and power) we have reached the morning, by You we had reached the evening, by You we live, by You we wil die, and to You will be our emergence (from graves).[63]

————

Abu Hurayrah رضي الله عنه *reported that the Prophet* ﷺ *recommended to say in the morning 100-times:*

«سُبْحانَ اللَّهِ وَبِحَمْدِه.»

SubhanAllāhi wa-bihamdih.

Exalted be Allah, and praise be to Him.

The Prophet ﷺ *further indicated that whoever says this, his sins will be forgiven, even if they exceed the foam of the sea. And no one will come on Resurrection Day with better deeds — except for a person who says the same or more.*[64]

————

---

[63] Muslim, Abu Dawood and others
[64] Muslim (2692), Abu Dawood and others

'Abdullah Bin 'Umar رضي الله عنه *reported that the Prophet* ﷺ *would not leave off saying the following supplication in the evening:*

«اللهُمَّ إِنِّي أَسْأَلُكَ العَافِيَةَ فِي الدُّنيا والآخِرَةِ. اللهُمَّ أَسْأَلُكَ العَفْوَ والعَافِيَةَ فِي دِينِي ودُنْيَايَ وأَهْلِي ومالِي. اللهُمَّ اسْتُرْ عَوْرَاتِي وآمِنْ رَوعاتِي. اللهُمَّ احْفَظْنِي مِن بَين يَدَيَّ ومِن خَلْفِي، وعن يَمِينِي وعن شِمالِي، ومِن فَوْقِي، وأَعُوذُ بِعَظَمَتِكَ أَن أُغْتَالَ مِنْ تَحْتِي. »

Allāhumma inni asalukal 'aafiyata fid-dunya wal-akhirah. Allāhumma asalukal 'afwa wal-afiyata fie dieni wa-dunyaya wa-ahli wa-maali. Allāhummastur 'awrati wa-amin rawa'ati. Allāhummahfasni min bayni yadayya wa-min khalfi, wa- an yamini wa-'an shimali, wa-min fauqi, wa-authu bi-'asamatika an ughtaala min tahti.

O Allah, I ask You for well-being in this first and the next. O Allah, I seek Your pardon and well-being in regard to my religion, life, family, and wealth. O Allah, cover my weaknesses and ease my fear. O Allah, protect me from in front of me and behind me, from my right and left sides, and from above me; and I seek refuge in Your greatness that I may be attacked from underneath me.[65]

———

Anas رضي الله عنه *reported that the Prophet* ﷺ *told Fatimah* رضي الله عنه *to say in the evening:*

« يا حيُّ يا قيّومُ، بِرَحْمَتِكَ أَسْتَغِيثُ، أَصْلِحْ لِي شَأْنِي كُلَّهُ، ولا تَكِلْنِي إِلَى نَفْسِي طَرْفَةَ عَيْنٍ أَبداً. »

Ya hayyu, ya qayyum, bi-rahmatika astaghith. Aslih li shani kullah, wala takilni ila nafsi tarfata 'aynin abada.

---

[65] Abu Dawood, an-Nasa'I and others

O You who are ever Living and Watchful, through Your mercy I appeal for help, so rectify all of my affairs, and do not relinquish me to myself for even as little as a blink of an eye.[66]

———

Abu ad-Darda' رضي الله عنه *said that Allah alleviates all concerns for a person who says seven times in the evening:*

«حَسْبِيَ اللهُ لَا إِلٰهَ إِلاَّ هُوَ، عليْهِ توَكَّلْتُ، وهُوَ ربُّ العَرْشِ العَظيمِ.»

Hasbiy Allāhu la ilaha ilia huwa 'alayhi tawakkalt, wa-huwa rabb ul-arsh il-azlm.

Sufficient for me (as helper and protector) is Allah; there is no (true) god except Him; upon Him I rely, and He is the Lord of the great Throne.[67]

———

Abu Bakrah رضي الله عنه *reported that he heard the Prophet* ﷺ *say three times in the evening:*

«اللّٰهُمَّ عافِني في بَدَني، اللّٰهُمَّ عافِني في سَمْعي، اللّٰهُمَّ عافِني في بَصَري، لا إِلٰهَ إِلاَّ أَنتَ. اللهُمَّ إِنّي أَعوذُ بكَ مِن الكُفْرِ والفَقْرِ، اللّٰهُمَّ إِنّي أَعوذُ بكَ مِن عذابِ القَبْرِ.»

Allāhumma 'afini fie badani, Allāhumma 'afini fie sam'i, Allāhumma 'afini fie basari, la ilaha illa ant. Allāhumma inni authu bika min al-kufri wal-faqr, Allāhumma inni authu bika min 'athab il-qabr.

---

[66] an-Nasa'i and al-Bazzar
[67] Ibn 'Asakir, Ibn us-Sunni and others

O Allah, grant me well-being in my body, my hearing, and my eyesight. There is no (true) god but You. O Allah, I seek Your protection from disbelief (or ingratitude) and poverty, and I seek Your protection from the torment of the grave.[68]

'Abd ur-Rahman Bin Abza رضي الله عنه *reported that the Prophet* ﷺ *used to say in the evening:*

«أَمْسَيْنا عَلى فِطْرَةِ الإسلامِ، وكلِمَةِ الإخْلاصِ، وعلى دينِ نَبِيِّنا مُحَمَّدٍ، وعَلى مِلَّةِ أبينا إبراهيمَ، حَنيفاً وما كانَ مِنَ الْمُشْرِكينَ.»

Amsayna 'ala fitratil-Islam, wa-kalimat il-ikhlas, wa- 'ala dini nabiyyina Muhammad, wa-ala millati abina Ibrahima hanifan wamaa kana minal-mushrikien.

We have reached the morning while we are upon the pure nature (fitrah) of Islam, and the word of Sincerity (i.e., the Shahadah), and the religion of our Prophet Muhammad, and the creed of our forefather Ibrahim: He was pure in faith and was not of those who joined partners with Allah. [69]

Khawlah Bint Hakim رضي الله عنه *reported that she heard the Prophet* ﷺ *say: „Whoever stops at a place (for camping or rest) and says:*

أَعُوذُ بِكَلِمَاتِ اللهِ التَّامَّاتِ مِنْ شَرِّ مَا خَلَقَ

A'udhu bi kalimaat-illaahit-taammaati min sharri maa khalaq.

I seek refuge in Allah's complete words from all that He created.

---

[68] Abu Dawud, an-Nasa'i and others
[69] Ahmad, at-Tabarani and others

nothing will harm him while he stays at that place."[70]

'Abdullah Bin 'Amr رضي الله عنه reported that the Prophet ﷺ said: "When one of you is terrified during his sleep, let him say:

«أَعُوذُ بِكَلِمَاتِ اللهِ التَامَّةِ مِن غَضَبِهِ وَشَرِّ
عِبَادِهِ، وَمِن هَمَزَاتِ الشَّيَاطِينِ وَأَن يَحَضُرُونِ»

A'uthu bikalimat-illah it-tammati min ghadabihi wa sharri ibadih, wa min hamazat ish-shayatieni wa an yahduruun.

I seek refuge in Allah's complete words from His anger, from the evil of His creation, and from the spurring of the devils or that they be present with me.[71]

Going to bed early

Ibn 'Abbas and Abu Burazah رضي الله عنه reported that Allah's Messenger ﷺ prohibited sleeping before the 'Isha prayer or chatting after it.[72]

'Aishah رضي الله عنه reported that Allah's Messenger ﷺ used to sleep in the early part of the night, and wake up (for worship) during its last part.[73]

---

[70] Muslim (2708), an-Nasa'i and others
[71] Abu Dawood, at-Tirmithi and others
[72] Tabarani
[73] Bukhari (1146), Muslim (739) and others

Cleaning hands and teeth before going to sleep

Abu Hurayrah and Ibn 'Abbas رضي الله عنه *reported that the Prophet* ﷺ *said: „Whoever has residues of greasy food on his hand and goes to sleep without washing them off, then if something happens to him during the night (like a sting or bite), let him blame none but himself."*[74]

'Aishah and Ibn 'Abbas رضي الله عنه *reported that the Prophet* ﷺ *said: „Siwak*[75] *purifies the mouth and pleases the Lord."*[76]

Taking ablution

Ibn 'Umar رضي الله عنه *reported that the Prophet* ﷺ *said: „When a person goes to sleep with taharah (state of ritual purity), an angel stays in his covers. If he wakes up at any time of the night, the angel says, "O Allah, forgive Your servant because he slept with taharah.""*[77]

———

Mu'ath Bin Jabal رضي الله عنه *reported that the Prophet* ﷺ *said: „Whenever a Muslim goes to sleep while he has taharah and while extolling Allah, and then wakes up during the night and asks Allah for any good from this life or the hereafter, He will grant it to him."*[78]

---

[74] Abu Dawood, at-Tirmithi and others
[75] A twig of a desert scrub
[76] Ahmad, an-Nasa'i
[77] Ibn Hibban and at-Tabarani
[78] Abu Dawood, Ibn Majah and others

Ibn 'Umar رضي الله عنه reported that he asked the Prophet ﷺ: „May one of us go to sleep while he is junub' (ritual greater impurity)? The Prophet ﷺ replied: „Yes, but after performing wudu — if he wishes."[79]

How one sleeps

Al-Bara, Huthayfah, and Hafsah رضي الله عنه reported that when the Prophet ﷺ went to bed, he put his hand under his right cheek.[80]

———

Al-Bara Bin 'Azib رضي الله عنه reported that the Prophet ﷺ told him: „When you go to bed, perform a wudu like that for the prayer, then lie on your right side."[81]

———

Abu Hurayrah رضي الله عنه reported that the Prophet ﷺ saw a man lying down on his stomach, so he said: „Indeed, this is a manner of sleep that Allah dislikes."[82]

———

---

[79] Bukhari (287, 289, 290), Muslim (306) and others
[80] Bukhari (286, 288), Muslim (305) and others
[81] Bukharl (247), Muslim (2710) and others
[82] Tirmithi, Ibn Hibban and others

'Ali Bin Shayban, Jabir and another companion رضي
الله عنه reported that the Prophet ﷺ said: „Whoever
sleeps on a house's roof that has no rail (or cover)
and then falls and dies, we take no responsibility for
him."[83]

———

Ibn 'Umar رضي الله عنه reported that the messenger of
Allāh ﷺ prohibited solitude, which is to sleep lonely
or travel lonely. [84]

———

Abu Sa'id al-Khudri رضي الله عنه reported that the
Prophet ﷺ said: „Let not a man look at another
man's 'awrah (or nakedness), nor a woman at
another woman's. And let not a man sleep under
the same cover with another man, nor a woman
with another woman.[85]

———

Abu Hurayrah رضي الله عنه reported that the Prophet ﷺ
said: „Whenever a person goes to sleep without
extolling Allah that will be a source of regret for him
on Resurrection Day. And whenever a person sits in
a sitting in which he does not extoll Allah, that will
be a source of regret for him on Resurrection Day."[86]

———

[83] Abu Dawood, Tirmithi and others
[84] Ahmad
[85] Muslim (338), Abu Dawood and others
[86] Abu Dawood, an-Nasa'i

'Abdullah Bin 'Amr reported that the Prophet ﷺ said: „Satan comes to a person when he is ready to sleep, and makes him fall asleep before he finishes saying them (the athkar)." [87]

———

When you go to bed, recite Ayat ul-Kursi (al-Baqarah 255) until you conclude it. Allah will then set a protector over you, and no devil would approach you until the morning. [88]

———

'Uqbah Bin 'Amir رضي الله عنه reported that the Prophet ﷺ said: „O 'Uqbah Bin 'Amir, should I not teach you Suras that nothing similar to them was revealed in the Tawrah (Torah), the Zabur (Psalms), the Injil (Gospel), or the Quran? They are: "Qul huw-allahu ahad", "Qul authu bi rabb-il-falaq" and "Qul authu bi rabb-in-Nas". Let not a night come upon you and you go to bed without reciting them." [89]

———

'Aishah رضي الله عنه reported that when Allah's Messenger ﷺ went to bed, he would bring the palms of both hands together, and breathe into them while reciting "Qul huw-allahu ahad", "Qul authu bi rabb-il-falaq", and "Qul authu bi rabb-in- Nas". He would then rub with them whatever he could reach of his body, starting with his head, face, and the

---

[87] Abu Dawood, Tirmithi
[88] Ibn Khuzaymah and others
[89] Ahmad

front part of his body. He would do this three times. When he was too ill, he asked me to do this for him.[90]

———

'Aishah رضي الله عنه reported that the Prophet ﷺ did not use to sleep before he recited Surat ul-Isra and Surat uz-Zumar.[91]

———

Jabir رضي الله عنه reported that the Prophet ﷺ did not used to sleep before he recited Surat us-Sajadat and Surat ul-Mulk.[92]

———

Ali رضي الله عنه reported that his wife Fatimah رضي الله عنه complained that her hands ached from using the hand mill. Hearing that her father ﷺ had received some war prisoners, she requested from him a servant. The Prophet ﷺ came to her house and addressed her and 'Ali saying: Should I not teach you both something better than what you requested? When you go to bed, say tasbih thirty-three times, tahmid thirty-three times, and takbir thirty-four times. This would be better for you than a servants.[93] *(This is why this dhikr is also called Dhikrul Fatimah, which one also should recite after the obligatory prayer.)*

---

[90] Bukhari (5017, 5748), Abu Dawood and others
[91] Tirmithi, Ahmad and others
[92] an-Nasa'i, at-Tirmithi and others
[93] Bukhari (3113, 3705, 5361, 6318), Muslim (2727) and others

'Abdullah Bin 'Amr رضي الله عنه *reported that the Prophet ﷺ said: „Satan comes to a person while he is ready to sleep, and makes him fall asleep before he finishes saying them; and he comes to him after the prayer, and reminds him of something he needs to do instead of saying them."[94]*

––––––

Abu Bakr as-Siddiq, Abu Hurayrah and other companions رضي الله عنه *reported that the Prophet ﷺ teached them to recite the following before going to bed:*

«اللّهُمّ عالِمَ الغَيْبِ والشّهادةِ، فاطِرَ السّماواتِ والأرضِ، رَبّ كُلّ شَيءٍ وَمَليكَهُ، أشْهَدُ أنْ لآ إلَهَ إلاّ أنتَ، أعوذُ بكَ مِنْ شَرّ نَفْسي، ومِنْ شَرّ الشّيطانِ وشِرْكِهِ، وأنْ أقْتَرِفَ عَلى نَفْسي سوءاً أو أجُرّهُ إلى مُسْلِمٍ.»

Allāhumma 'alimal ghaybi wash-shahadat, fatir as-samawati wal-ardh, rabba kulli shay in wa-malikah, ash-hadu ala ilaha illa ant, authu bika min sharri nafsi, wa-min sharr ish-shaytani wa-shirkih, wa-an aqtarifa 'ala nafsi suan au ajurrahu ila Muslim.

O Allah, Knower of the ghayb and witnessed worlds, Creator of the heavens and earth, Lord and Sovereign of all things: I bear witness that there is no (true) god except You. I seek Your protection from the evil of myself, from the evil and shirk of Satan, and from that I would commit harm against myself or direct it toward another Muslim.[95]

––––––

––––––––––––––––––––

[94] Abu Dawood, at-Tirmithi and others
[95] Abu Dawood, at-Tirmithi and others

Anas رضي الله عنه *reported that the Prophet* ﷺ *said:*
„*Whoever says when he goes to bed:*

الْحَمْدُ لله الذي كَفَاني وآواني،

الْحَمْدُ لله الذي أطعَمَني وسَقاني،

الْحمدُ لله الذي مَنَّ علَيَّ وأفضَلَ.

اللهُمَّ إني أسألُكَ بعِزّتِكَ أنْ تُنَجِّيَني مِنَ النَّارِ

Al-hamdu lillahil-latju kafani wa-awani; al-hamdu lillahil-lathi at amani wa-saqani; al-hamdu lillahil- lathi manna 'alayya wa-afdal. Allāhumma inni as-aluka bi-is-satika an tunajjiyani minan-nar.

Praise be to Allah who sufficed me and gave me abode; praise be to Allah who fed me and gave me drink; praise be to Allah who favored me with His generosity. O Allah, I ask You, by Your dignity, to save me from the Fire.

Whoever says this should indeed have praised Allāh with all forms of praise of the whole creations."[96]

———

Abu Hurayrah رضي الله عنه *reported that the Prophet* ﷺ *instructed to say the following when going to bed, and indicated that whoever says it, his sins will be forgiven, even if they were as much as the foam of the sea:*

«لا إلَهَ إلَّا اللّٰهُ وَحدَهُ لا شَريكَ لَه، لَهُ الملكُ ولَه الحَمدُ، وَهُوَ عَلَى كُلِّ شَيءٍ قَديرٌ. لا حَوْلَ ولا قُوَةَ إلاَّ باللّٰه العَليِّ العَظيم، سُبْحانَ اللّٰهِ، والْحَمْدُ لله، ولا إلَهَ إلاَّ اللّٰهُ، واللّٰهُ أكْبَرُ.»

---

[96] al-Bayhaqi, al-Hakim and others

La ilaha illAllāh, wahdahu la sharika lah, lahul-mulku, wa-la hul-hamdu, wa-huwa 'ala kulli shayin qadir. La haula wala quwata ilia billahil-'Aliyy il-Azim. Subhan Allāhi, wal-hamdu lillahi, wa-la ilaha illAllāhu, wallāhu akbar.

There is no (true) god except Allah, alone and without any partners. To Him belongs the dominion, He deserves all praise, and He is capable of everything. There is no power or might except from Allah, the Supreme, the Great; exalted be Allah; all praise be to Allah; there is no (true) god but Allah; Allah is the Greatest.[97]

Huthayfah and al-Bara رضي الله عنه *reported that when the Prophet* ﷺ *went to sleep, he would put his hand under his right cheek and say:*

$$ \text{« بِاَسْمِكَ اللهُمَّ أموتُ وأَحْيا . »} $$

Bismik-Allāhumma amutu wa-ahya.

With Your Name, O Allah, I die and live.[98]

Abu Hurayrah رضي الله عنه *reported that the Prophet* ﷺ *said: „When a person goes to sleep, Satan ties three knots over the back of his head, blowing into each knot while saying, "You have a long night, so sleep on." If this person wakes up and extolls Allah, one knot loosens. If he performs wudu, another knot loosens. And if he prays, the third knot loosens, so that he becomes lively, good-natured, and successful; otherwise, he gets up in the morning ill-natured, lazy, and unsuccessful.[99]*

---

[97] an-Nasa'I, Ibn Hibban
[98] al-Bukhari (6312, 6314, 6324), Muslim (2710), and others
[99] al-Bukhari (1142, 3269), Muslim (776), and others

'Abdullah Bin Mas'ud رضي الله عنه *reported that a man was mentioned to the Prophet* ﷺ *who slept until the morning without getting up for prayer. The Prophet* ﷺ *said: Satan has urinated in this man's ears.* "[100]

———

Ibn 'Umar رضي الله عنه *reported that the Prophet* ﷺ *would not sleep without the siwak next to him. When he woke up, he would start off by using the siwak.*[101]

———

Abu Hurayrah رضي الله عنه *reported that the Prophet* ﷺ *said: „When one of you wakes up and performs wudu, he should rinse his nose and blow it three times, because the Devil sleeps upon his nose.*[102]

The Blessing of the night-prayer

Abu Hurayrah رضي الله عنه *reported that the Prophet* ﷺ *said: „Our Lord descends every night to the lowest heaven when only one third of the night has remained. He says, "Who is there invoking Me, so that I may answer him? Who is there asking Me, so that I may give him? Who is there seeking My forgiveness, so that I may forgive him?"*[103]

———

---

[100] al-Bukhari (1144, 3270), Muslim (774), and others
[101] Ahmad and Ibn Nasr
[102] al-Bukhari (3295), Muslim (238), and others
[103] Tirmithi, an-Nasa'i, and al-Hakim

Their (the believers') sides forsake their beds, to invoke their Lord in fear and hope; and they spend out of what We bestowed on them. [as-Sajadah 16]

———

Lo! Those who keep from evil will dwell amid gardens and watersprings, taking that which their Lord giveth them; for lo! Aforetime they were doers of good; they used to sleep but little of the night, And ere the dawning of each day would seek forgiveness. [Ad-Dhariyat 15-18]

———

Abu Umamah رضي الله عنه reported that the Prophet ﷺ said: „I urge you to perform, qiyam at night, because it was the consistent way of the righteous people who preceded you, it is a means of coming closer to Your Lord, it is a means of expiating your wrongdoings, and it is a restraint against sinning.[104]

Abu Hurayrah reported that the Prophet ﷺ said: „The best of prayers after those prescribed, are those prayed in the depth of the night."[105]

———

'Aishah رضي الله عنه reported that the Prophet's ﷺ qiyam prayer was so long that his legs swelled and his feet cracked. They asked him, "Why should you do this, O Allah's Messenger, when all of your sins, past and future, have been forgiven?" He replied:

---

[104] Tirmithi, at-Tabarani, and others
[105] Muslim (1163) and Ahmad

"Should I not be a servant who is perpetually grateful (to Allah)?"[106]

———

'Abdullah Bin 'Amr رضي الله عنه reported that the Prophet ﷺ said: "Whoever prays qiyam reciting ten verses, he will not be recorded among the negligent. Whoever prays qiyam reciting one hundred ayat, he will be recorded among the devout. And whoever prays qiyam reciting one thousand ayat, he will be recorded among those with a multitude of good deeds."[107]

———

'Aishah رضي الله عنه reported that the Prophet ﷺ said: „Take upon yourselves only deeds that you can (consistently) maintain, for, by Allah, Allah is never bored (i.e., never stops accepting your deeds) until you are (by interrupting your heavy worship)."[108]

Huthayfah and al-Bara رضي الله عنه reported that the Prophet ﷺ used to say when he woke up:

«الْحَمْدُ لِلَّهِ الذِي أَحْيَانا بَعْدَمَا أَمَاتَنا، وَإِلَيْهِ النُّشُورُ.»

Al-hamdulillah-hil-lasi ahyana b'ada maa amaatana, wa-ilayhin-nushur.

Praise be to Allah who resurrected us after He made us die. And to Him will be the (people's) emergence (from graves).[109]

---

[106] al-Bukhari (1130, 4836, 6471), Muslim (2819), and others
[107] Abu Dawood and Ibn Hibban
[108] al-Bukhari (43) and Muslim (785)
[109] Bukhari (6312, 6314, 6324), Muslim (2710), and others

How to destroy a Buhul?

When it comes to destroying a Buhul, there are a number of things to consider.

The following equipment is required:

- A tray so that everything stays together and nothing falls on the floor.

- A long-neck gas lighter - as they are often used to light grills.

- A suitable container for burning the Buhul. If no stainless steel cylinder is available, an old pan will do.

- Gloves

If the Buhul is wrapped in something, one also needs:

- A pair of pliers and scissors, and perhaps other tools to open the cladding.

- Eye protection is recommended.

If the Buhul contains nodes, one also needs:

- A loose razor blade

If the method requires Ruqya water, one also needs:

- A bowl of tap water

Before one starts: It is recommended to constantly recite al-Falaq and an-Naas throughout the process from beginning to end.

Opening the Buhul:

- Open the Buhul in the middle of the tray to collect everything that might fall from it.

- Open the Buhul carefully so that you do not get hurt, and the Buhul will not dissolve while you open it (although this can happen sometimes).

- Many Buhul are wrapped in metal or leather, and often with wax to seal them. Use pliers, scissors and other suitable tools to remove the metal or leather case. Keep all parts on the tray so that nothing is lost.

- Wax can be removed by gently melting it with the gas lighter.

- Once the Buhul is open, it should be checked for nodes. Any knots should be cut completely with the razor blade.

When the Buhul is engraved in metal:

- When the Buhul is engraved in metal, e.g. a ring, the engravings must be rendered unrecognizable, e.g. with the aid of a file or some other tool until there are no visible markings.

- Once all the markings are removed, dispose of them in clean soil, in a place not often used by humans, or by throwing into a river or the sea.

When the Buhul is written on paper:

- If the Buhul is written on paper and given for burning (i.e., the sorcerer said it needs to be burned at a certain time), it should be destroyed by the water method.

- If the writing of the Buhul consists of soluble ink (usually yellow, saffron-based ink or pink color), it should also be destroyed by the water method.

- Any other Buhul should be destroyed using the Fire method.

- If in doubt, combine the two by first using the water method, then drying the Buhul and destroying it with the burning method.

The Burning Method:

- Place the Buhul in a suitable container to burn it and to collect all ashes and residues.

- The Buhul should be incinerated in a place that is not often visited by people to reduce the risk of someone being harmed.

- Use a long-necked gas fired burner to burn the Buhul as completely as possible, avoiding inhaling the smoke. If you feel that something is going to stop you from burning the Buhul, try to recite Koran constantly while you burn it.

- Bury the ash and residue in clean soil, together with the contents of the tray used to open the Buhul.

The water method:

- Take a bowl of water and recite al-Fatihah and the last three Suras of the Qur'an. If one has already prepared Ruqya water, one can use it.

- Place the bowl with the water on the tray so that everything is held together and the water is not spilled.

- Put the Buhul into the water and rub off any soluble ink.

- Take the Buhul out of the water and break it or rip it as best as it can be done. The remnants along with the water are to be disposed of in a place that is not often visited by people to reduce the risk of harming someone, or throwing it into a river or the sea.

Are Ta'wies allowed?

Some people use *Ta'wies* (verses of the Qur'an or Du'as, written on something, and then hung over the door or around the neck etc) to protect themselves from 'Ain, black magic, or Jinn, or even for healing purposes.

Then there are Ta'wies, where one does not know exactly what is written on them, and which should not only protect, but also bring luck with lottery, in order to find daily a new sex partner, to revenge oneself etc.

While it is obvious that the second kind of Ta'wies is haram and falls into the category "Buhul", there is doubt about the first kind. There are both arguments for and against.

The majority of scholars are of the opinion that this first kind is not haram, but not recommended (*makruh* - disapproved) because it could easily lead to haram. For if one believes that the Ta'wies has some power in itself, then it is shirk.

This, of course, is the case with anything else too. If one believes that e.g. pills against headache, or Ruqya or whatsoever has some power on its own, then that's also shirk. All might and power come from Allāh alone.

But could we say it is haram if somebody argues: "The calligraphy is a nice decoration and reminds me of Allah, and by remembering Allah I am better protected against the shayateen"?

I would like to stay out of a debate about the legal aspect, and only tell about my own experience. A friend of mine, a professor at the University of Gorontalo and a good Raqi, had once asked a Jinn where he lived. The Jinn replied that he lived in Ayat ul-Kursi, the verse of the throne. A rather surprising answer, since the verse of the throne is usually the best weapon against Jinn!

It turned out that the verse of the throne of which the Jinn spoke was hanging on the patient's wall, and that the patient evidently attributed some power to the verse of the throne when it is hung up in the house like that! And since this is shirk, it attracted the Jinn!

The danger that if we use a Ta'wies attribute power and strength to it and thus commit shirk, is quite real. And I do not know of any Raqi, who would ever have prescribed Ta'wies for protection. I therefore agree with the opinion of the majority of the scholars and advise against it.

Jinn in other religions and cultures

In all cultures and epochs one finds the belief in Jinn in various forms. Sometimes they are called elementary spirits, sometimes fairies, sometimes demons, or even gods.

And on the day when He will gather them all together, He will say unto the angels: Did these worship you? They will say: Be Thou Glorified. Thou [alone] art our Guardian, not them! Nay, but they worshipped the Jinn; most of them were believers in them. [Saba 40-41]

Thus, if e.g. Buddhists pray in front of Buddha, they bow before the Jinn / devil who lives in the statue. In principle, therefore, they are doing what a sorcerer does, and are therefore enabled by Jinn to do "super-natural" things.

Take a look at what the Buddhist-Shaolin monks can do: For example, an iron rod is bent by pressure on the neck, without causing an injury, or a needle thrown through a glass wall. Scientifically "proven", because recorded by camera, but scientifically "explained"?

To this day, science has no explanation how structures such as Stonehenge or the statues on the Easter Islands were built. There are also no convincing theories about the pyramids, which is mainly due to the fact that no mass graves were found near the pyramids, but which should exist if they would have been built in a conventional way with an army of workers. If we exclude extraterrestrials as builders, only the Jinn remain.

Buddhists and Hindus believe in reincarnation. They take as proof, among other things, the way in which the Dalai Lama, the head of the Tibetans, is elected, or rather is found. He is regarded as *tulku*, an enlightened being that incarnates several hundred years (14 lives). Unlike ordinary people, he can choose the human in whom he reincarnates. The task of the other lamas is to find the child into which the Dalai Lama has incarnated. 2-3 years after the death of the Dalai Lama, the search begins.

In earlier years, the lamas traveled to the oracle lake Lhamo Lhatso, a holy place where a spirit (!) lives, called *Palden Lhamo*. There, the lamas meditated and saw in visions and dreams the place where they had to look for the new incarnation. At this place then, they put small objects of the old Dalai Lama (such as his robe, his eating bowl etc) in front of the children and mixed them with lots of other items, and the child who picked all the right items had to be the incarnation of the old Dalai Lama.

But apparently, not the old Dalai Lama did incarnate himself, but the Jinn who lived in him, and who beomes hundreds of years old![110]

---

[110] The fact that the Dalai Lama is in no way a Bodhisattva, an enlightened being, illustrates the merciless exploitation of the Tibetans before the invasion of the Chinese. 3% of the Tibetans factually ruled over the masses, who belonged to the monasteries and the few rich, and who had to pay enormous levies. There was slavery, massive poverty and hunger. Tibet was by no means the paradise on earth as the Dalai Lama likes to portray it, and in which the Europeans are so fond of believing. The Dalai Lama and his family owned 40,000 people, who farmed 27 land estates. Only in the monasteries were schools, the normal people had no health care, and the infant mortality rate was at 50%! The life expectancy of the average Tibetan was 35 years only! All this explained by evil karma, for which the people themselves were to blame, e.g. if they dared to critizise the ruling class. Contrary to the propaganda broadcasted in the West, the Chinese were welcomed by the people, because the slavery and misery were ended. In the late 1990s, the Dalai Lama had to admit, what he had always denied, namely the payments and his links with the CIA. The "incarnated enlightened

If in Hawaii formerly somebody wanted to become king, he had to show that he could surf. A surfboard of about 5m lenght was carved from the Wili Wili tree. Before the tree got cut, however, one had to sacrifice a kumu fish at the roots of the tree to ask the gods for permission. Obviously, the Jinn who lived on the tree should be soothed. This kind of sacrifice or soothing of the ethereal beings who live on trees can be found in many cultures. In Islam it is sufficient to say "*Bismillah*" before the tree is cut.

How shamans and medical practitioners use Jinn for treatment, we had already mentioned in the preface. Christians also have "miracle healings" and even "Miracle Healing Crusades", where in large assemblies people are healed in series and shout "Hallelujah". The method is the same as that of the shamans and the exorcist of the Vatican: A commander of the Jinn, normally a powerful Ifrit, kicks out the Jinn in the body of the patient responsible for the illness, on which the patient recovers and praises Jesus who allegedly has healed him. Patient healed, but on the way to hell!

Just go to Lourdes and look at all the wheelchairs and crutches left standing! There, then, it is not Jesus who heals, but supposedly his mother. The little girl Bernadette Soubirous saw eighteen times the Virgin Mary in the grotto of Massabielle in Lourdes, and is said to have freed up with her own hands a spring whose water cures the sick. During these "cures", not only Jinn play a role, but of course also placebo / autosuggestion. Every year, this place is visited

---

being" had deceived and lied for decades. He is a handsome figure among other Nobel Peace Prize winners such as Aung San Suu Kyi, Myanmar's president, where the Rohingya are slaughtered, or Menachim Begin, who was personally involved in the killing of Palestinians.

by six million pilgrims from all continents, who spend altogether 2.5 billion euros.

Yes, shirk has always been a good source of income, which is why the Quraish so vehemently rejected the teachings of Muhammad ﷺ, because he ruined their business. After all, the 350 gods in and around the Kaaba attracted pilgrims from all over Arabia and brought considerable wealth to the Quraish.

Who worships something other than Allāh, prays to *taghut*, thus ultimately Satan, and the devil who lives in these idols:

And make mention [O Muhammad] in the Scripture of Abraham. Lo! he was a saint, a prophet. When he said unto his father: O my father! Why worshippest thou that which heareth not nor seeth, nor can in aught avail thee? O my father! Serve not the devil. Lo! the devil is a rebel unto the Beneficent. [Maryam 41, 42, 44]

The gods, especially the sun god (behind whom Satan hides), always demanded human sacrifices:

- Mayas: Kulkulcan
- Babylon: Vul / Baal
- Romans: Volcan
- Egyptians: Osiris / Ra
- Greeks: Helios
- Aztecs: Tonatiuh
- Sumerians: Ea / Enki
- Assyrian: Shamash
- Hindus: Surya
- China: Tai-Yang-King

People, especially firstborn, were often sacrificed on what is now considered the symbol of mercy: the cross. And it is not surprising that under the sign of the cross more people died than under any other symbol.

The arrival of the cross in America on the sail of Columbus' ship Santa Maria, announced the extermination of 4/5 of the indigenous population. The rest of the world shared a similar fate during half a millennium of colonization.

Half of Europe was exterminated in the 30-year war between Catholics and Protestants. A good part of the population fell victim to the Inquisition, and was not only murdered, but also gruesomely tortured. Likewise the crusades did not honor the alleged symbol of mercy, but revealed once again that the human sacrifice of God's alleged son was in fact Satan worship and nothing else!

Yet they ascribe as partners unto Him the Jinn, although He did create them, and impute falsely, without knowledge, sons and daughters unto Him. Glorified be He and High Exalted above [all] that they ascribe [unto Him]. [Al-Anam 100]

About the author

Born in Aachen, Germany, in 1966, irreligious until the age of about 22, he began after some journeys and other profound experiences to study first esoteric and then religion in general intensively. At the age of twenty-four, he finally managed to flee the treadmill of German everyday life by trying to entrust himself to God. Since 1997 he lives with his wife and three children in Indonesia.

Contributors:

Muhammad Mustafa al-Jibaly – The Dreamer's Handbook

Sheik Muhammad Tim Humble (muhammadtim.com)

Sheik Abdur Raouf ben Halima (ruqyacentre.com)

Nuruddin al-Indonissy (nai-foundation.com)

Abu Haroon (ruqyasupport.com)

M.T. (quranheilung.de)

Other titles by the same author on Amazon:

The Fitnah of the Dajjal

With the help of modern technologies, a new, all-encompassing and all-controlling superorganism is created that fulfills the promise of Satan, which he gave man at the beginning of time: Apotheosis – becoming like God! The misled, globalized people who are made believe, they lived in the best and most progressive epoch of human history, are increasingly enslaved by a diabolic political and economic system, and by a certain perception of reality. While the creation is dying and the world at the brink of Armageddon, the individual has only one chance: Surrender to God!

Christianity from the perspective of Islam

Viewing things from a distance might make them appear quite different! Likewise Christianity, when seen from the viewpoint of Islam. This book invites to reflection. It offers new perspectives and inspiration for those who are not holding rigid to a dogma, but who give priority to the truth!

No Name Nomad: A quest for guidance

No Name Nomad describes the author's journey from an irreligious materialistic life to one full of meaning and closeness to God. He leaves his home-country and former life, trusting in God and His promise. He tries to get rid of all materialistic things and walks thousands of kilometres without money, passport and baggage, and finally finds his true identity on a little dugout in the middle of the Indian Ocean. The book describes the attempt to follow, without compromise, one's own intuitions and the inner guide. The author compares his intuitions and outer situations with waves. These waves one has to recognize and 'to ride' if they should bring one to new shores because the rational analysis of a situation and its logical conclusion never suffice to adjust oneself to the constant flow of life and God's will. Surfing becomes him a symbol, and the author starts it also on the material plane to better understand its laws. This brings him to an island south-west of Sumatra where are some of the highest waves in the world. There he gets an English translation of the Koran and the waves get a name: Hidaya.

Printed in Great Britain
by Amazon

44122182R00128